MESSI VS RONALDO

202 TRIVIA QUESTIONS, STORIES AND FACTS IN A DUAL BIOGRAPHY

FAME FOCUS

CONTENTS

INTRODUCTION

Welcome to the ultimate showdown in football history – *Messi VS Ronaldo*. This book is more than just a collection of trivia; it's a journey through the careers of two of the greatest footballers of our time – Lionel Messi and Cristiano Ronaldo.

In these pages, you'll discover a treasure trove of stories, facts, and insights that delve deep into the lives and careers of these iconic athletes. From the streets of Rosario and Madeira to the pinnacle of global football, Messi and Ronaldo have captivated fans worldwide with their extraordinary skills, relentless ambition, and contrasting styles.

As you read their stories and flip through the trivia questions, you'll find yourself immersed in their world - their early struggles, their rise to fame, their epic battles on the field, and their profound impact off it. This book is not just about stats and records; it's about understanding what makes Messi and Ronaldo transcendental figures in sports history.

Whether you're a die-hard Messi fan, a devoted Ronaldo supporter, or simply a lover of football, this book promises to enlighten, entertain, and challenge you. So, prepare to dive into an exhilarating exploration of skill, resilience, and the sheer love for the beautiful game.

Let the duel begin!

1

INSIDE THE WORLD OF FOOTBALL

Before we delve into the remarkable journeys of Lionel Messi and Cristiano Ronaldo in football, it is crucial to first comprehend the broader football world that has served as a stage for their awe-inspiring careers. In this section, we will examine key facets of football that have been integral to their stories. We will explore the significance of the Ballon d'Or, the thrill of La Liga, the prestige of the UEFA Champions League, the passion of El Clásico, the global allure of the FIFA World Cup, the rich history of Copa America and the dynamic energy of the Premier League.

Understanding these competitions and awards is vital to fully appreciating the journeys and triumphs of both Messi and Ronaldo. These events are more than just tournaments or accolades; they symbolize the pinnacle of a sport adored by millions worldwide. As we discuss Messi and Ronaldo in the pages to follow, grasping this background will enable us to see the full extent of their impact on football and its celebrated legacy.

Ballon d'Or

The Ballon d'Or is one of the most prestigious individual awards in the world of football. It's an annual accolade presented by France Football magazine to the best male footballer in the world, as voted on by a panel of international journalists, national team coaches, national team captains, and managers.

The award has a long history, dating back to 1956 when it was first introduced. Originally, it was limited to European players playing for European clubs, but the eligibility criteria were expanded to include players from all around the world, regardless of where they play, in 1995.

The Ballon d'Or recognizes outstanding individual performances in a calendar year, taking into account a player's contributions to their club and national team. The criteria for selecting the winner include skill, consistency, leadership, and impact on the game. The award is a symbol of excellence in football and is highly coveted by players, as it represents recognition of their talent and achievements on the field.

El Clásico

"El Clásico" is more than just a football match; it's a legendary rivalry between FC Barcelona and Real Madrid, representing a historic and intense contest that has captivated fans since the early 20th century. This rivalry, known for being one of the most anticipated in world football, involves much more than the sport itself. Matches between Barcelona and Real Madrid are global events, marked by high stakes, intense emotions, and unparalleled competition. These games are cultural phenomena that often divide families, cities, and even nations along footballing lines.

The global appeal of "El Clásico" is immense, drawing attention from fans around the world. It's not only a display of extraordinary player talent but also a showcase of the unique footballing philosophies and traditions of the two clubs. The rivalry has been graced by football legends like Lionel Messi, Alfredo Di Stéfano, and Johan Cruyff, each adding to the match's prestige with memorable performances.

Beyond the pitch, "El Clásico" holds significant cultural importance in Spain, embodying the nation's diverse identities. Barcelona and Real Madrid represent more than just football clubs; they symbolize regional pride and political nuances, with Barcelona often associated with Catalonia and Real Madrid with the Spanish capital.

The matches are events where passion, skill, and drama converge, captivating both football enthusiasts and casual viewers. Whether played at Barcelona's Camp Nou or Madrid's Santiago Bernabéu, these stadiums transform into stages where some of football's greatest stories unfold, making "El Clásico" a true spectacle in the world of sports.

Premier League

The Premier League, established in 1992, is England's elite professional football league and one of the world's most historic and widely followed football competitions. It has become a hallmark of English football, known for its global appeal and competitive nature.

Featuring 20 clubs, the Premier League's season runs from August to May, with each club playing 38 matches against all others, both home and away. Celebrated for its diversity and unpredictability, the league sees a blend of varying styles and philosophies, leading to a dynamic and thrilling brand of football. Known for its fast-paced, end-to-end play, the Premier League is especially noted for its focus on attacking football.

The league has cultivated an enormous international following, attracting fans globally with its high production values, extensive broadcasting, and world-class talent, making it one of the most-watched sports leagues worldwide. Iconic clubs like Manchester United, Liverpool, Chelsea, Arsenal, and Manchester City, each with fervent fan bases, add to the league's allure. Historic rivalries, such as the "North West Derby" between Liverpool and Manchester United, inject additional drama and history into the league.

Premier League clubs have consistently shown excellence in European competitions, often featuring prominently in the UEFA Champions League and UEFA Europa League. Beyond the field, the Premier League is deeply embedded in English culture and society, resonating with millions of fans. Football forms an integral part of the nation's heritage, with Premier League matches being of great significance to local communities.

La Liga

La Liga, or the Spanish Football League, has a storied history that spans nearly a century, tracing its roots back to its establishment in 1929. It stands as one of Europe's oldest football leagues, steeped in tradition and significance within the Spanish football landscape.

La Liga consists of 20 teams that undergo a rigorous season from August to May, each team playing 38 matches - one at home and one away against every other team. Scoring in this league is based on wins (three points), draws (one point), and losses (zero points), all contributing to the race for the championship. Known for its captivating and technical style of play, La Liga is home to famous clubs like FC Barcelona and Real Madrid, whose intense rivalry in "El Clásico" attracts global attention. The league's appeal extends far beyond Spain, captivating fans worldwide with its top-tier talent and high-quality football. On the European stage, La Liga clubs, including Barcelona, Real Madrid, and Atletico Madrid, have consistently excelled, cementing their status as European football powerhouses in tournaments like the UEFA Champions League and UEFA Europa League. Within Spain, La Liga holds a significant cultural place, with football being a deeply rooted passion. League matches are a key part of the country's sports and social calendar, underlining football's profound influence on Spanish society. Furthermore, La Liga has been instrumental in expanding football's popularity globally, propelling Spanish football to a prominent position and spreading the love for the game to various corners of the world.

Copa America

The Copa America, established in 1916, stands as a testament to South America's rich football history, being the oldest international football competition in the world. This prestigious tournament has been instrumental in shaping the continent's football landscape, deeply rooted in tradition and passion.

The Copa America is a biennial event that brings together the top national teams from South America in a competitive and fervent showcase of football excellence. It is celebrated for highlighting the continent's rich footballing traditions and talents, captivating fans across South America and beyond with each edition. The tournament is renowned for its intense rivalries, with matches often charged with strong emotions. Iconic matchups like Brazil vs. Argentina, known as the "Superclásico de las Américas," and Uruguay vs. Argentina in the "Clásico del Río de la Plata," are legendary and resonate deeply with fans.

While primarily a South American event, the Copa America has attracted a global audience, thanks to its high level of play and the presence of world-class talent. It offers football enthusiasts worldwide the chance to witness some of the sport's best players in action.

UEFA European Championship

Since its first edition in 1960, the UEFA European Championship, commonly known as the Euro, has been a pivotal event in the world of football, captivating fans with its rich history and showcasing Europe's finest national teams. As one of the most esteemed international football competitions, it has evolved significantly over the years. The competition format of the modern Euro includes 24 top national teams from UEFA member countries, divided into groups and then proceeding to knockout stages, culminating in the crowning of the European champion. The Euro is celebrated for its intense matches, tactical prowess, and the emergence of new football heroes, offering a stage where national pride and passion reach their zenith, creating unforgettable moments.

While the Euro is a European event, its appeal extends globally, attracting football enthusiasts worldwide. Its high-level play and world-class talent make it a highlight of the international football calendar. Over the years, the championship has witnessed a variety of winners, from football giants to unexpected underdogs, each contributing to the diverse tapestry of European football. More than just a sporting competition, the Euro holds a special place in European culture, symbolizing a celebration that unites nations and communities, fostering unity and pride. On the international football stage, the Euro's impact is profound. It offers teams a chance to compete against the best, with success in the tournament becoming a source of national pride and glory, thus playing a significant role in shaping the international football landscape.

FIFA World Cup

The FIFA World Cup represents the zenith of international football, having established itself as a historic and beloved event since its inception in 1930. Renowned as the most prestigious and widely viewed sporting event globally, the World Cup showcases top national teams from every continent.

More than just a football tournament, the World Cup is a worldwide celebration of the sport. Held quadrennially, it unites nations, cultures, and people from diverse backgrounds in their shared passion for football. This period is marked by a global pause, as football fever sweeps through countries, captivating the attention of people worldwide.

The competition within the World Cup is intense. Teams engage in a month-long contest that is a testament to national pride, with players showcasing their talent on the world's biggest stage. The format of the tournament encompasses group stages, knockout rounds, and culminates in the final, with each match carrying the potential to make history.

The World Cup has been the arena for the emergence of legendary players who have significantly influenced the sport. Icons such as Pelé, and Diego Maradona have graced this tournament, demonstrating extraordinary footballing prowess.

Beyond the realm of sports, the World Cup has a profound cultural impact. It fosters unity and camaraderie, often bringing together rival nations in a shared celebration. The event also allows host countries the opportunity to display their culture, traditions, and hospitality to a global audience.

The World Cup transcends being merely a sporting event; it is a global phenomenon. Attracting billions of viewers, sparking passionate discussions, and creating indelible memories, the tournament holds the unique power to inspire and unite people like no other event in the world.

2

MESSI'S LIFE

Early Years

The story of Lionel Andrés Messi Cuccitini, born on June 24, 1987, in Rosario, Argentina, is a tale of a football prodigy who overcame challenges to become a legend. Messi's journey began in a football-loving family, where his passion for the game was nurtured from a young age. His father, Jorge Messi, a local steel factory manager, played a crucial role in his early development, coaching Lionel and his brothers at the local club, Grandoli.

From a young age, around four, Messi's talent was evident. He joined Grandoli, where under his father's guidance, he honed his skills. His exceptional abilities soon became apparent, and at the age of 8, he joined Newell's Old Boys, a prominent club in Rosario, where he distinguished himself as a prodigious talent.

However, Messi's journey was not without obstacles. At around 10, he was diagnosed with idiopathic short stature, a growth hormone deficiency, which hindered his physical development. Despite this setback, Messi's family, particularly his mother Celia Cuccitini, provided unwavering emotional support. They approached River Plate, a major Argentinian football club, for assistance with his expensive growth hormone treatments. Unfortunately, River Plate couldn't fund his treatment either.

A pivotal moment came in 2000 when Messi, at 13, moved to Barcelona, Spain, with his family. FC Barcelona had offered to pay for his medical treatments and included him in their youth academy, La Masia. This move marked a new chapter in Messi's life, offering him the platform to showcase his talent on a larger stage. His initial contract with Barcelona, famously signed on a paper napkin, symbolized the club's immediate and decisive commitment to his extraordinary talent.

Lionel Messi's family played an integral role in his journey. He is the third of four children, with a significant age gap between him and his siblings. His older brother Rodrigo, born in 1979, manages Lionel's professional schedule. Matías, five years older, born in 1982, oversees Lionel's charitable foundation. His younger sister, María Sol, born in 1993, maintains a private life but shares a close bond with Lionel.

The Emergence at FC Barcelona

Lionel Messi's ascent in the world of professional football began in February 2002. At the tender age of 13, after joining Barcelona's prestigious youth academy, La Masia, a significant milestone was achieved when he was officially enrolled in the Royal Spanish Football Federation (RFEF). This crucial step not only legitimized his status as a player within the Spanish football system but also paved the way for a career that would later redefine the sport.

By June 2004, Messi's potential had crystalized into undeniable talent. Recognizing this, FC Barcelona signed him to his first official contract, solidifying his status as a professional player with the club. This moment marked the beginning of an era, one where Messi would soon become a household name in football.

Messi's first appearance for FC Barcelona's first team came on October 16, 2004, in a La Liga match against Espanyol. At just 17, stepping onto the field in the 82nd minute, he marked the beginning of what would be a historic debut in professional football. The following year, on May 1, 2005, Messi scored his first official goal for FC Barcelona in a match against Albacete Balompié. Coming off the bench, his skillful lob over the goalkeeper, assisted by Ronaldinho, was a clear indication of the extraordinary talent he possessed.

The 2004/05 season was a harbinger of success for Messi, as he won his first La Liga trophy with FC Barcelona. Although he made only 7 appearances, all as a substitute, and scored a single goal, his impact on the team was already becoming evident.

On November 2, 2005, Messi scored his first UEFA Champions League goal against Panathinaikos. His talent was further showcased in a match against Real Madrid in March 2007, where, at just 19, he became the youngest player to score a hat-trick in the tournament. The 2005-2006 season saw Messi win his first Champions League trophy with FC Barcelona, contributing one goal and one assist in six appearances, although missing the final against Arsenal due to injury.

A defining moment in Messi's early career occurred on March 10, 2007, in an El Clásico match against Real Madrid. At just 19 years old, Messi scored his first career hat-trick, resulting in a 3-3 draw. This performance etched his name in the history books, as he became the first player since Iván Zamorano to score a hat-trick in an El Clásico match. This feat not only underscored his emerging prowess but also highlighted his potential to become one of the greatest players in football history.

April 18, 2007, remains etched in football history, thanks to Messi's stunning goal in a Copa del Rey semi-final match against Getafe. Starting near the halfway line, he embarked on a breathtaking 60-meter sprint, weaving past five defenders before finishing with an angled shot. This goal is not just remembered as one of the best in football history but also revered by Barcelona fans as the finest in their club's storied history.

The 2008-2009 season was also a testament to Messi's growing influence and skill. He was instrumental in FC Barcelona's first-ever treble, securing La Liga, Copa del Rey, and the UEFA Champions League titles. His role as the top scorer in the Champions League during this period solidified his standing as one of the premier footballers on the global stage.

The 2011-2012 season was a showcase of Messi's goal-scoring prowess. He netted an astonishing 73 goals across all competitions for Barcelona, surpassing Gerd Muller's longstanding record for the most goals in a calendar year and earning his fourth consecutive Ballon d'Or.

March 7, 2012, saw Messi achieve an unprecedented feat in the UEFA Champions League. In a match against Bayer Leverkusen, he scored five goals – a record in the competition. This performance not only highlighted his exceptional skills but also set a new benchmark in Champions League history.

On March 20, 2012, Messi reached another career milestone, becoming Barcelona's all-time top scorer. At only 24, he broke Cesar Rodriguez's 57-year-old record by scoring a hat-trick against Granada, bringing his total to 234 goals for the club.

From 2013 to 2021, Lionel Messi continued to be a central figure in FC Barcelona, contributing significantly to the team's performances. During this period, he displayed consistency in goal-scoring and playmaking, maintaining his status as one of the top players globally. He played a key role in Barcelona's successes, including domestic league titles and notable achievements in European competitions. His influence on the team was characterized by a combination of individual brilliance and teamwork. However, the later years also witnessed some transitions and challenges within the club.

Messi's departure from Barcelona in 2021 marked the end of an era for the club and player, concluding a long and impactful association.

Paris Saint-Germain & Inter Miami

August 2021 marked the beginning of a new era for Messi as he completed a highly anticipated transfer to Paris Saint-Germain after a 21-year stint with Barcelona. Wearing the number 30 jersey, he formed a formidable attacking trio with Neymar and Kylian Mbappé, helping PSG secure the Ligue 1 title in his debut season. His performance with PSG showcased his continued football prowess, contributing both goals and assists, while his adaptability and skill set complemented the team's attacking style of play. His partnership with other star players in the squad became a focal point, significantly influencing the team's dynamics on the field.

Following his time at Paris Saint-Germain, Messi embarked on a new chapter with Major League Soccer club Inter Miami. This significant move in his illustrious career saw him signing a two-and-a-half-season contract, with the possibility of extending it further, potentially keeping him at the club until the 2026 season.

Performance Alongside Argentina

Throughout his football career, Lionel Messi has been a consistent and influential figure for the Argentine national team. From his early days, he demonstrated his talent and versatility on the international stage. Despite facing occasional criticism for not replicating his club success with Barcelona on the national team, he remained a key player, contributing to Argentina's campaigns in various tournaments. His commitment to representing his country has been a notable aspect of his football journey.

Messi's international prowess was on full display on August 23, 2008, at the Beijing Olympic Games. In the final against Nigeria, held in the iconic Bird's Nest stadium, he provided a crucial assist, leading Argentina to a 1-0 victory and their second consecutive Olympic football gold medal. This win marked the first time since Uruguay in 1924 and 1928 that a team had achieved back-to-back Olympic golds in football.

In the 2014 FIFA World Cup held in Brazil, Messi took center stage for Argentina's national team. He led his country to the World Cup final, contributing four goals and numerous assists. Though Argentina finished as runners-up, Messi's extraordinary performances earned him the Golden Ball award, further cementing his legacy as one of the greatest players in the sport's history.

In the 2015 Copa América, Messi led Argentina to the final, showcasing his exceptional skill and leadership. However, the tournament ended in heartbreak as Argentina lost to Chile in a penalty shootout. Despite the defeat, Messi's outstanding performances throughout the tournament earned him the Player of the Tournament award.

In July 2021, Messi realized a lifelong dream by leading Argentina to victory in the Copa América. Defeating Brazil 1-0 in the final, Argentina claimed their first Copa América title in 28 years, and Messi won his first major international trophy. His instrumental role throughout the tournament led to him being named Player of the Tournament and sharing the Golden Boot.

In the 2022 FIFA World Cup final at Lusail Stadium, Messi's legendary status was further cemented. Making a record 26th World Cup finals appearance, he played a pivotal role in the thrilling final. Scoring Argentina's opening goal and again in extra-time, he led his team through a dramatic match against France. The game, tied 3-3 after extra time, was decided in a penalty shootout, with Argentina triumphing 4-2, thus ending a 36-year wait for the World Cup trophy. Messi's extraordinary performances, including 7 goals and 3 assists, earned him the Golden Ball as the tournament's best player.

International Recognition & Awards

Messi's talent garnered international recognition in 2005. At the FIFA World Youth Championship, he clinched both the Golden Ball, as the tournament's best player, and the Golden Shoe, as the top scorer with six goals. However, his journey with the Argentine national team had a rocky start. In a friendly against Hungary in 2005, Messi was sent off just one minute after entering the field, sparking debates about the red card's fairness. Despite this setback, he scored his first international goal in a friendly against Croatia on March 1, 2006.

In 2009, at just 22 years old, Messi won his first Ballon d'Or, an award recognizing the world's best player, following his pivotal role in Barcelona's treble-winning season. His dominance in football continued in the following years, retaining the Ballon d'Or in 2010 and then again in 2011, 2012, and 2015. Messi's dominance in the sport was further cemented in December 2019 when he won his sixth Ballon d'Or, setting a new record in the award's history. This honor was a testament to his consistent high-level performances, including scoring 50 goals and providing 18 assists in just 59 games. Messi continued to make history with his seventh and eighth Ballon d'Or wins in 2021 and 2023, respectively, further solidifying his status as one of football's all-time greats.

Messi's exceptional talent was again recognized on November 29, 2021, when he won his seventh Ballon d'Or. The following year, in the 2022 Finalissima at Wembley Stadium, Messi demonstrated his brilliance on the international stage. Argentina's victory over Italy, with Messi contributing two assists, underscored his enduring influence and skill in high-stakes matches.

Messi's dominance in football extends to the global stage, as evidenced by his two FIFA World Cup Golden Ball awards. These awards, won in 2014 and 2018, are a testament to his exceptional skill and impact at the World Cup, the pinnacle of international football. In both tournaments, Messi's performances were pivotal in driving Argentina's campaigns, with his ability to influence games being particularly noteworthy. These accolades not only recognize his individual brilliance but also his capacity to elevate his national team's performance on the world's biggest football stage.

Messi's global influence is highlighted by his five FIFA World Player of the Year titles, won in 2009, 2010, 2011, 2012, and 2015. This recognition places him among the most celebrated footballers in history, emphasizing his impact on the sport at an international level.

In his home country of Argentina, Messi's exceptional talent has been recognized with him being named the Argentine Footballer of the Year 13 times. This honor underscores his lasting impact on football in Argentina and his status as a national icon.

Noteworthy Records

La Liga's All-Time Top Scorer: On November 22, 2014, Messi made football history by becoming the all-time top scorer in La Liga. In a mesmerizing performance against Sevilla, he scored a hat-trick, surpassing Telmo Zarra's 59-year-old record with 252 goals. This achievement not only highlighted his scoring prowess but also firmly entrenched him in the annals of football history.

The Fastest Hat-trick: Messi's record of 57 career hat-tricks is a demonstration of his consistent excellence. He holds the record for the fastest hat trick in La Liga history, achieving this feat in just 12 minutes during a match against Rayo Vallecano on March 8, 2015.

A Milestone in El Clásico: A significant moment in Messi's career occurred on April 23, 2017, when he scored his 500th goal for Barcelona in all competitions. This milestone was achieved in dramatic fashion during an El Clásico match against Real Madrid, where his overtime goal sealed a crucial 3-2 victory.

Surpassing Pelé's Record: On December 22, 2020, Messi achieved another historic milestone by becoming the top goalscorer with a single club, surpassing Pelé's record of 643 goals with Santos. Messi's 644th goal, scored in a victory over Real Valladolid, broke a record that had stood for 46 years.

Record-Breaking Ballon d'Or Wins: Lionel Messi's illustrious career is marked by multiple Ballon d'Or victories, a prestigious individual accolade awarded annually by France Football. His first triumph came in 2009, followed by consecutive wins in 2010 and 2011. Messi continued his dominance, claiming the award in 2012 and 2015. After a brief hiatus, he secured the Ballon d'Or once again in 2019, setting a new record with six wins. Messi added to this remarkable feat with his seventh Ballon d'Or in 2021 and an eighth in 2023, reaffirming his status as one of the greatest footballers in history. Each victory reflects his consistent excellence and enduring impact on the global football stage.

Holder of 41 Guinness World Records: Messi's name is associated with an impressive 41 Guinness World Records, a testament to his extraordinary achievements in football. Notable records include winning the most Man of the Match awards at the FIFA World Cup (11), being the first person to assist in five different FIFA World Cups, making the most FIFA World Cup appearances as a captain (19), and having the most appearances in FIFA World Cup tournaments by a male player, participating in 5 different editions. These records not only highlight his consistency and excellence on the global stage but also his leadership and influence in the sport.

Playing Style

Over the years, Messi's playing style has undergone a remarkable transformation. Initially celebrated as a nimble and skillful winger at FC Barcelona, he seamlessly combined extraordinary dribbling skills with precise finishing. Gradually, he evolved into a more central attacking role, often operating as a 'false nine,' merging his playmaking abilities with prolific goal-scoring. During his tenure at Paris Saint-Germain, Messi continued to adapt, embracing a more creative midfield role while maintaining his scoring threat. His expressed desire to continue playing at the highest level into his late 30s underscores his dedication to maintaining top physical fitness and performance standards throughout his career.

Messi's signature move, earning him the nickname "La Pulga" (The Flea), showcases his exceptional agility and quickness. Characterized by rapid changes in direction while maintaining close control of the ball, this move has become a hallmark of his playing style. His low center of gravity, coupled with extraordinary balance and dribbling skills, enables him to weave through tight spaces and evade multiple defenders, often leaving them bewildered in his wake.

Remarkable Skills

Lionel Messi's career has been marked by a series of impressive achievements and skills that highlight his impact on football.

Free-Kick Expertise: Messi's prowess in free-kicks is evident in his 65 successful conversions. This skill has been a fundamental aspect of his play, contributing significantly to his team's success.

Consistent Scorer: Remarkably, Messi has scored goals in every minute of a football match, demonstrating his consistent threat in front of the goal throughout the entire duration of a game.

Physical Attributes and Scoring Versatility: Despite his height of 5 feet 7 inches (1.7 meters), Messi's performance has been on par with, or surpassed, taller players, challenging the notion that physical stature is a key determinant of success in football. His ability to score with various parts of his body is notable, with 23 headed goals and 75 right-footed goals, adding to his dominant left-footed scoring ability.

Penalty Conversion: Messi's effectiveness is also seen in penalty situations, where he converted 77 penalties for Barcelona, showcasing his skill in high-pressure scenarios.

Goal Distribution: His scoring distribution is balanced, with 215 goals from the left field, 215 from the right, and 104 from the center. Notably, 385 of his goals have come from within the 6-yard box, reflecting his proficiency in close-range scoring. Additionally, he has demonstrated his ability to score from long-range, with 24 goals from beyond the 18-yard box.

Providing for Teammates: Beyond scoring, Messi has recorded 205 assists during his time at Barcelona, for example, indicating his ability to contribute to his team's offensive play beyond just scoring goals.

Training Regimen & Diet

Messi's exceptional agility and speed on the field are products of a structured and disciplined workout plan. His training regimen is designed to optimize both linear and multidirectional speed, incorporating exercises like lunges, hamstring stretches, pillar skips, skipping ropes, and squats. Agility is a key focus, with diagonal hurdles and cone drills forming integral parts of his routine. Each session concludes with proper hydration and a cooldown jog, emphasizing the importance of recovery in his physical preparation.

His lifestyle choices, particularly his diet, play a fundamental role in his performance. Messi follows a diet focused on hydration and whole foods, avoiding sugar and fried foods. His typical meal includes roasted chicken with root vegetables, with a limited intake of meat during training periods. He emphasizes the importance of protein shakes and water for digestion, underscoring his commitment to maintaining top physical fitness.

Rituals & Preferences

Messi is known to have a few superstitions that are part of his pre-game rituals. One such superstition is entering the field with his right foot first. He also wears the same shin guards that his grandmother bought him as a child, a touching homage to her influence in his early life. Before stepping onto the pitch, Messi typically kisses his tattoo of his mother's lips, further paying tribute to her and carrying her presence with him in every game.

Messi's iconic goal celebration, pointing towards the sky, is a deeply personal tribute to his late grandmother, Celia. She was instrumental in nurturing his passion for football during his early years. Her encouragement played a significant role in his development as a young footballer. Despite her passing in 1998, Messi's celebration ensures that her memory and influence continue to be a part of his journey, reflecting the deep bond they shared.

In a candid interview with Paris Saint-Germain, Messi revealed his preference for the role of a second striker. He articulated a fondness for playing centrally, just behind the lead striker, a position where he feels most at home. Messi's inclination for this role stems from his desire to be continuously involved in the game, underlining his passion for contributing actively to his team's play. His statement, "I like to always be in contact with the ball," reflects his playmaking ethos and his enjoyment in orchestrating the game, making crucial passes, and setting up goals.

Personal Life & Interests

Lionel Messi's illustrious career is a blend of remarkable professional achievements and personal elements that offer deeper insights into his character and preferences, contributing to his multifaceted persona.

His personal life, particularly his relationship with Antonela Roccuzzo, is a demonstration of his grounded and loving nature. Both hailing from Rosario, Argentina, they met in childhood and began dating in their teens. Their relationship culminated in a grand wedding in 2017, attended by numerous celebrities and football stars. The couple has three sons, Thiago, Mateo, and Ciro, who have shown an early interest in soccer, much to the anticipation of fans worldwide.

During his iconic tenure with FC Barcelona, the city became a second home for Messi and his family. They immersed themselves in the local culture and community, embracing everything the Catalan capital had to offer beyond the football pitch.

Exploring another facet of Lionel Messi's diverse interests, his passion for art is evident in his collection, which includes works by Catalan surrealist Joan Miró, known for their abstract and playful nature. This collection offers insight into Messi's appreciation for art that challenges reality.

Concerning Messi's tattoos, they are more than just body art; they are deeply personal. On his left shoulder, he has a tattoo of his mother's face, symbolizing her unwavering support throughout his life and career. Additionally, he has tattooed the name of his firstborn son, Thiago, on his calf, reflecting the strong bond and immense love he holds for his son.

Lionel is also known for being a pet lover. He often shares his affection for dogs on social media, particularly his Dogue de Bordeaux, a breed known for its loyalty and affectionate nature. His social media posts frequently feature pictures and videos of his beloved pet. Beyond his love for pets, Messi has a musical side too. He plays the guitar during his leisure time, using music as a form of relaxation and a way to unwind from the demands of his high-profile career.

Native to Rosario, Argentina, Lionel Messi primarily communicates in Spanish. Throughout his extensive tenure at FC Barcelona, Messi became familiar with Catalan, the predominant language in the region. Despite this, he has not yet acquired proficiency in additional languages like English, often opting to express himself in Spanish during public appearances and interviews. This choice reflects his comfort with his native language and cultural roots, despite his global presence.

In navigating the often extroverted landscape of professional sports, Lionel Messi's renowned introverted personality sets him apart. Known for his inherent shyness and reserved demeanor, particularly evident in the early stages of his career, Messi's distinctive approach to fame is reflected in his modest goal celebrations and a preference for a private life, shielded from the constant media spotlight. This unique aspect of his personality, in contrast to the more common public personas of professional athletes, has endeared him to fans who value his commitment to football and personal integrity over the allure of celebrity status.

Philanthropy

In the latter stages of Lionel Messi's career, a period seamlessly intertwined with his personal life and off-field contributions, monumental achievements unfold alongside a deep commitment to family and philanthropy. Messi's impact transcends the boundaries of football, extending far beyond the pitch. The genesis of this broader influence lies in the Leo Messi Foundation, a testament to his dedication to improving the lives of disadvantaged children, especially in healthcare and education. Through his foundation, Messi has spearheaded various initiatives, including the construction of schools and medical facilities. Furthermore, his active engagement in charitable activities beyond the foundation encompasses contributions to disaster relief and healthcare projects. These humanitarian efforts have garnered numerous accolades, underscoring Messi's role as a positive influence both on and off the field.

Off the Field Ventures

Lionel Messi's career, marked by staggering achievements on the field, is complemented by his ventures into fashion, hospitality, and art, as well as his record-breaking performances. Beyond his football prowess and endorsements, Messi expanded his influence into the fashion industry with "The Messi Store." This venture reflects his personal style and taste, offering a range of clothing and apparel that resonates with his fans and fashion enthusiasts.

Messi's passion for design is further showcased through "The Messi Collection," a collaboration with architect Luis Galliussi. This unique furniture line blends aesthetics, functionality, and comfort, allowing fans to incorporate Messi's distinctive style into their homes.

Messi's entrepreneurial spirit also extends to the culinary world with the "Bellavista del Jardín del Norte" restaurant chain in Argentina. These establishments are celebrated for their delightful ambiance and a menu rich in Argentine culinary traditions, attracting both locals and international visitors and contributing to Messi's portfolio outside of football.

In Barcelona, Messi's partnership with the Majestic Hotel Group led to the creation of the "Majestic Messi" hotel. Located in the heart of Barcelona, this luxury hotel caters to tourists seeking cultural experiences and premium service, thus significantly contributing to the local tourism and economy.

On a broader international scale, Messi is renowned for his partnerships with major brands such as Adidas, Pepsi, and Huawei. These endorsements not only contribute significantly to his income but also establish him as a prominent global icon in the sports industry.

Fun, Random Facts

• Messi's admiration for former Argentine playmaker Pablo Aimar is a notable aspect of his football journey. Growing up, Messi looked up to Aimar, and their paths crossed in La Liga, leading to a memorable encounter where Aimar gifted his shirt to a 17-year-old Messi. This gesture left an indelible mark on Messi and symbolized his admiration for Aimar. Interestingly, Aimar later became an assistant coach for the Argentina national team, contributing to their success in the 2022 World Cup, adding a unique dimension to their relationship.

• During his time at Barcelona's La Masia academy, Messi caught the attention of Arsenal's former manager Arsene Wenger. Wenger's interest in signing Messi highlights the early recognition of his talent, but Messi's commitment to Barcelona saw him decline the offer and continue his growth with the Catalan club.

• In a unique tribute to his football prowess, Messi's left foot was immortalized in a 25-carat gold cast. This symbol of his impact on the sport was valued at $5.3 million and sold to support those affected by the 2011 tsunami in Japan, demonstrating how his legacy extends beyond the pitch.

• Despite his numerous awards, Messi has never won the Golden Foot Award, an accolade recognizing players' achievements and personality.

• In his career, Messi has received three red cards, two with Argentina and one with FC Barcelona, rare incidents in an otherwise disciplined career.

• An interesting aspect of Messi's personal life is his family connection to former Barcelona teammate Bojan Krkic. They are fourth cousins, with shared ancestors dating back to the 19th century in Catalonia. This connection adds a familial dimension to their professional relationship and their shared football journey.

• Away from the limelight of professional football, Messi displays endearing traits that make him relatable to fans. Former Argentina teammate Pablo Zabaleta shared light-hearted anecdotes, revealing that Messi is less adept at playing FIFA video games, often choosing Chelsea as his preferred team. Zabaleta also humorously commented on Messi's modest culinary skills and dancing abilities, portraying a side of Messi that is more personal and distinct from his football identity.

• In a high-profile legal case, Messi faced a 21-month prison sentence for tax fraud, which was later converted into a fine by Spanish courts. He was required to pay €252,000, which equates to €400 for each day of the original sentence. This case arose from accusations of defrauding Spain of €4.1 million between 2007 and 2009 through the use of tax havens to conceal earnings from image rights. Similarly, his father, Jorge Messi, also faced legal repercussions, with his 15-month sentence being replaced by a €180,000 fine.

• Messi's digital representation in the FIFA video game series mirrors his real-life success. From FIFA 06 to FIFA 23, his ratings have consistently been among the highest, reflecting his status as one of the top players in the world. Notably, Messi has appeared on the cover of soccer video games a record 12 times.

• Messi is synonymous with the number 10 jersey, a symbol of playmaking excellence and leadership in football. He inherited this number from Ronaldinho at FC Barcelona in 2008, a gesture that symbolized the passing of the baton to Messi as the team's leading playmaker and a key figure in football. At Paris Saint-Germain, Messi initially chose number 30, reminiscent of his first professional number at Barcelona, before returning to the iconic number 10. This jersey number has become a significant part of Messi's identity, representing his status as one of the greatest players in the history of the sport.

Digital Presence

Lionel Messi's life extends far beyond the football pitch, embodying a richness and diversity reflective of his multifaceted career. His journey is characterized by distinct symbols, unique habits, a robust digital presence, and a lifestyle that significantly contributes to his on-field success.

Surpassing a remarkable milestone, Messi has garnered over 100 million followers on Instagram, underscoring his global popularity and influence. Within the digital realm, his account seamlessly weaves together personal moments with his family, highlights from his illustrious football career, and diverse endorsements, providing fans with a captivating glimpse into both his professional and personal spheres.

TRIVIA QUESTIONS

1. What is Lionel Messi's full birth name?

a) Lionel Andrés Di María

b) Lionel Messi

c) Lionel Andrés Messi

d) Lionel Andrés Messi Cuccitini

2. What was Lionel Messi's father's occupation?

a) Football Coach

b) Steel Factory Manager

c) Professional Footballer

d) School Teacher

3. What role did Lionel Messi's mother play in his development?

a) She was his first football coach

b) She managed his early career

c) She provided strong emotional support

d) She was a professional athlete

4. How many siblings does Lionel Messi have?

a) One

b) Two

c) Three

d) Four

5. At what age did Lionel Messi start playing soccer?

a) 3 years old

b) 4 years old

c) 5 years old

d) 6 years old

6. Which club did Lionel Messi join at age 8?

a) FC Barcelona

b) River Plate

c) Boca Juniors

d) Newell's Old Boys

7. What medical condition was Lionel Messi diagnosed with at the age of 10?

a) Idiopathic short stature

b) Asthma

c) Osteoporosis

d) Anemia

8. Which football club did Messi's family approach for help with his medical treatments?

a) Boca Juniors

b) River Plate

c) Atlético Madrid

d) Independiente

9. At what age did Lionel Messi move to Barcelona, Spain?

a) 10

b) 11

c) 12

d) 13

10. How was Messi's initial contract with FC Barcelona signed?

a) On a formal contract paper

b) In a legal office

c) On a paper napkin

d) Digitally

11. At what age was Lionel Messi officially enrolled in the Royal Spanish Football Federation (RFEF)?

a) 11

b) 12

c) 13

d) 14

12. When did Messi sign his first official contract with FC Barcelona?

a) May 2003

b) June 2004

c) July 2005

d) August 2006

13. When did Lionel Messi make his official debut for FC Barcelona's first team?

a) October 2003

b) November 2004

c) October 2004

d) September 2005

14. When did Messi score his first official goal for FC Barcelona?

a) April 2005

b) May 2005

c) June 2005

d) July 2005

15. In which season did Messi win his first La Liga trophy with FC Barcelona?

a) 2003/04

b) 2004/05

c) 2005/06

d) 2006/07

16. Which awards did Messi win at the FIFA World Youth Championship in 2005?

a) Golden Boot and Silver Ball

b) Golden Shoe and Silver Ball

c) Golden Ball and Golden Shoe

d) Silver Ball and Silver Shoe

17. Against which team did Messi make his debut for the Argentine national team?

a) Brazil

b) Hungary

c) Croatia

d) Portugal

18. When did Messi score his first UEFA Champions League goal?

a) October 2005

b) November 2005

c) December 2005

d) January 2006

19. In which season did Messi win his first Champions League trophy with FC Barcelona?

a) 2004-2005

b) 2005-2006

c) 2006-2007

d) 2007-2008

20. In which match did Messi score his first career hat-trick?

a) Against Espanyol

b) Against Arsenal

c) Against Real Madrid

d) Against Chelsea

21. On which date did Lionel Messi score a goal often regarded as one of the best in football history in a Copa del Rey match against Getafe?

a) April 16, 2007

b) April 18, 2007

c) April 20, 2007

d) April 22, 2007

22. In which season did Messi help FC Barcelona achieve their first-ever treble?

a) 2006-2007

b) 2007-2008

c) 2008-2009

d) 2009-2010

23. When did Messi play a crucial role in Argentina's Olympic gold medal victory at the Beijing Games?

a) 2006

b) 2008

c) 2010

d) 2012

24. At what age did Lionel Messi win his first Ballon d'Or?

a) 20

b) 21

c) 22

d) 23

25. In which year did Messi win his second consecutive Ballon d'Or?

a) 2008

b) 2009

c) 2010

d) 2011

26. How many consecutive years did Messi win the Ballon d'Or from 2009?

a) Two

b) Three

c) Four

d) Five

27. When did Messi score five goals in a single UEFA Champions League match?

a) March 5, 2012

b) March 7, 2012

c) March 9, 2012

d) March 11, 2012

28. How many goals did Messi score in the 2011-2012 season, breaking Gerd Muller's record?

a) 68

b) 70

c) 73

d) 75

29. At what age did Messi become Barcelona's all-time top scorer?

a) 22

b) 23

c) 24

d) 25

30. In which FIFA World Cup did Messi lead Argentina to the final and win the Golden Ball award?

a) 2010

b) 2014

c) 2018

d) 2022

31. When did Lionel Messi become the all-time top scorer in La Liga?

a) November 2013

b) November 2014

c) November 2015

d) November 2016

32. What was the outcome of the 2015 Copa América final for Argentina?

a) Victory in regular time

b) Victory on penalties

c) Defeat in regular time

d) Defeat on penalties

33. When did Messi score his 500th goal for Barcelona?

a) April 2017

b) May 2017

c) June 2017

d) July 2017

34. How many times has Messi won the Ballon d'Or as of December 2019?

a) Four

b) Five

c) Six

d) Seven

35. When did Messi surpass Pelé's record to become the top goalscorer with a single club?

a) December 2019

b) December 2020

c) January 2021

d) February 2021

36. What achievement did Messi accomplish in the Copa América in July 2021?

a) Winning the Golden Boot

b) Winning his first major international trophy

c) Scoring the winning goal in the final

d) All of the above

37. In what year did Messi transfer to Paris Saint-Germain (PSG)?

a) 2020

b) 2021

c) 2022

d) 2023

38. Which squad number did Messi initially choose at PSG?

a) 10

b) 19

c) 30

d) 33

39. How many Ballon d'Or awards had Messi won by November 2021?

a) Six

b) Seven

c) Eight

d) Nine

40. In which event did Messi play a pivotal role for Argentina against Italy in 2022?

a) UEFA Champions League

b) Copa América

c) Finalissima

d) World Cup

41. How many World Cup finals appearances had Messi made by the 2022 FIFA World Cup?

a) 24

b) 25

c) 26

d) 27

42. In which league did Messi sign after leaving Paris Saint-Germain (PSG)?

a) English Premier League

b) La Liga

c) Major League Soccer (MLS)

d) Serie A

43. How did Lionel Messi and Antonela Roccuzzo first meet?

a) At a football match

b) Through mutual friends

c) As children in Rosario

d) In Barcelona

44. In which year did Lionel Messi marry Antonela Roccuzzo?

a) 2015

b) 2016

c) 2017

d) 2018

45. How many sons do Lionel Messi and Antonela Roccuzzo have?

a) One

b) Two

c) Three

d) Four

46. Which city served as a second home for Lionel Messi during his time at FC Barcelona?

a) Madrid

b) Rosario

c) Barcelona

d) Paris

47. What is the primary focus of the Leo Messi Foundation?

a) Sports training for youth

b) Healthcare initiatives for children

c) Disaster relief efforts

d) Providing football equipment

48. In addition to his foundation, what other charitable activities has Messi been involved in?

a) Environmental conservation

b) Animal rights activism

c) Disaster relief and healthcare

d) Political campaigns

49. What type of brands has Messi endorsed?

a) Automotive and luxury goods

b) Sportswear and technology

c) Fast food and beverages

d) Financial services and banking

50. What was Messi's role in Argentina's victory in the 2022 FIFA World Cup final?

a) Scoring a hat-trick

b) Assisting the winning goal

c) Scoring in the penalty shootout

d) Goalkeeping in the shootout

51. What type of brand did Lionel Messi launch in the fashion industry?

a) A luxury watch brand

b) A sports apparel brand

c) A clothing and apparel brand

d) A footwear brand

52. What is the name of the restaurant chain owned by Lionel Messi and his family in Argentina?

a) Messi's Delicacies

b) Argentine Flavors by Messi

c) Bellavista del Jardín del Norte

d) El Rincón de Messi

53. What unique aspect is associated with the "Majestic Messi" hotel in Barcelona?

a) Football-themed decorations

b) A museum dedicated to Messi

c) Emphasis on exclusivity and elegance

d) A sports complex with football fields

54. Which artist's works are prominently featured in Lionel Messi's art collection?

a) Pablo Picasso

b) Salvador Dalí

c) Joan Miró

d) Frida Kahlo

55. In La Liga, at what age did Lionel Messi receive a shirt as a gift from Pablo Aimar?

a) 15

b) 17

c) 20

d) 22

56. What type of artwork does Lionel Messi's collection predominantly feature?

a) Classical portraits

b) Abstract and playful pieces

c) Renaissance sculptures

d) Modernist installations

57. What is "The Messi Collection" known for?

a) A series of sports memorabilia

b) A unique line of watches

c) A distinctive furniture line

d) A collection of football kits

58. How many hat-tricks has Lionel Messi scored throughout his career?

a) 47

b) 57

c) 67

d) 77

59. What is Messi's record for the fastest hat-trick in La Liga?

a) 10 minutes

b) 12 minutes

c) 15 minutes

d) 20 minutes

60. How many free-kick goals has Messi scored?

a) 55

b) 60

c) 65

d) 70

61. In which minutes of a football match has Lionel Messi scored goals?

a) Only in the first half

b) Only in the second half

c) From the 1st to the 45th minute

d) Every minute, from the first to the last

62. How tall is Lionel Messi?

a) 5 feet 5 inches (1.65 meters)

b) 5 feet 7 inches (1.70 meters)

c) 5 feet 9 inches (1.75 meters)

d) 5 feet 11 inches (1.80 meters)

63. How many goals has Messi scored using his head?

a) 13

b) 23

c) 33

d) 43

64. How many goals has Messi scored with his right foot?

a) 55

b) 65

c) 75

d) 85

65. How many penalties has Messi converted for Barcelona?

a) 57

b) 67

c) 77

d) 87

66. From which field positions has Messi scored exactly 215 goals each?

a) Left and right fields

b) Center and right fields

c) Left and center fields

d) Behind the midline and left fields

67. How many of Messi's goals were scored from within the 6-yard box?

a) 285

b) 385

c) 485

d) 585

68. How many goals has Messi scored from beyond the 18-yard box?

a) 14

b) 24

c) 34

d) 44

69. How many assists has Messi recorded during his time at Barcelona?

a) 105

b) 205

c) 305

d) 405

70. In the digital realm, how does Messi's Instagram account offer a glimpse into his life?

a) Strictly professional moments

b) Exclusive family moments

c) Personal and professional moments

d) Highlights of endorsements only

71. How does Messi's approach to fame differ from the common public personas of professional athletes?

a) He seeks constant media attention

b) He maintains a private life

c) He avoids football commitments

d) He embraces celebrity status

72. What is Lionel Messi's signature move, earning him the nickname "La Pulga" (The Flea)?

a) A powerful header

b) A long-range shot

c) Exceptional agility and quick changes in direction

d) A sliding tackle

73. According to Messi, what reflects his playmaking ethos and enjoyment on the field?

a) Scoring spectacular goals

b) Making crucial passes and setting up goals

c) Defending aggressively

d) A preference for playing on the wings

74. How many FIFA World Player of the Year titles has Messi won?

a) 3

b) 4

c) 5

d) 6

75. How many times has Messi been named Argentine Footballer of the Year?

a) 10 times

b) 11 times

c) 12 times

d) 13 times

76. What unique tribute was made to Messi's left foot?

a) A statue in Barcelona

b) A solid 25-carat gold cast

c) A signature shoe line

d) An imprint at Camp Nou

77. Which prestigious football award has Messi never won?

a) Ballon d'Or

b) Golden Foot award

c) FIFA World Player of the Year

d) UEFA Best Player in Europe

78. How many red cards has Messi received in his career?

a) One

b) Two

c) Three

d) Four

79. Which club did Arsene Wenger try to sign Messi for?

a) Manchester United

b) Arsenal

c) Chelsea

d) Real Madrid

80. What is the family connection between Messi and Bojan Krkic?

a) Second cousins

b) Third cousins

c) Fourth cousins

d) Not related

81. How many times has Messi been awarded the FIFA World Cup Golden Ball?

a) Once

b) Twice

c) Three times

d) Never

82. What position does Messi prefer to play, as stated in his interview with PSG?

a) Winger

b) Striker

c) Central midfielder

d) Second striker

83. What is one of Messi's lesser-known skills according to his former teammate Pablo Zabaleta?

a) Cooking

b) Dancing

c) Playing FIFA on PlayStation

d) Playing guitar

84. Messi's goal celebration, pointing to the sky, is a tribute to whom?

a) His father

b) His grandmother

c) His mother

d) His son

85. Which former Argentine player did Messi idolize as a young football enthusiast?

a) Diego Maradona

b) Gabriel Batistuta

c) Pablo Aimar

d) Juan Román Riquelme

86. What significant tribute does Messi have tattooed on his left shoulder?

a) His father's portrait

b) His mother's face

c) His son's name

d) A football

87. One of Messi's superstitions involves how he enters the field. What does he do?

a) Ties his shoelaces twice

b) Enters with his right foot first

c) Touches the grass before playing

d) Wears a specific wristband

88. What milestone did Messi achieve on Instagram?

a) 50 million followers

b) 75 million followers

c) 100 million followers

d) 150 million followers

89. What type of dog does Lionel Messi own?

a) Labrador Retriever

b) Dogue de Bordeaux

c) German Shepherd

d) Golden Retriever

90. Aside from football, what musical talent does Messi possess?

a) Singing

b) Playing the guitar

c) Playing the piano

d) Drumming

91. How is Messi's signature move characterized?

a) Slow and deliberate

b) Rapid changes in direction with close ball control

c) Long, powerful strides

d) Aerial acrobatics

92. How many times has Messi appeared on the cover of video game franchises like FIFA and eFootball?

a) 8 times

b) 10 times

c) 12 times

d) 15 times

93. What is the focus of Lionel Messi's diet?

a) Low-carb, high-protein

b) Vegan

c) Hydration and whole foods

d) High-carb, low-fat

94. Messi primarily communicates in which language?

a) English

b) Catalan

c) Spanish

d) French

95. Which exercise is NOT part of Messi's workout plan?

a) Lunges

b) Squats

c) Pilates

d) Skipping ropes

96. What was the outcome of Lionel Messi's prison sentence for tax fraud?

a) It was fully served

b) Converted into community service

c) Converted into a fine

d) Pardoned by the Spanish government

97. Which jersey number did Messi inherit from Ronaldinho at FC Barcelona?

a) 7

b) 10

c) 30

d) 8

98. Which trait is Lionel Messi especially known for?

a) Extroverted personality

b) Introverted personality

c) Aggressive playing style

d) Flamboyant lifestyle

99. How many Guinness World Records does Lionel Messi hold?

a) 25

b) 31

c) 41

d) 50

100. Which of these statements best describes Messi's signature playing style?

a) Power and physical strength

b) Height and heading ability

c) Agility and quickness

d) Long-range shooting prowess

101. In his career, Messi transitioned from playing as a winger to which role?

a) Goalkeeper

b) Central defender

c) Creative midfielder

d) False nine

4

TRIVIA ANSWERS

1. d) Lionel Andrés Messi Cuccitini

2. b) Steel Factory Manager

3. c) She provided strong emotional support

4. c) Three

5. b) 4 years old

6. d) Newell's Old Boys

7. a) Idiopathic short stature

8. b) River Plate

9. d) 13

10. c) On a paper napkin

11. c) 13

12. b) June 2004

13. c) October 2004

14. b) May 2005

15. b) 2004/05

16. c) Golden Ball and Golden Shoe

17. b) Hungary

18. b) November 2005

19. b) 2005-2006

20. c) Against Real Madrid

21. b) April 18, 2007

22. c) 2008-2009

23. b) 2008

24. c) 22

25. c) 2010

26. c) Four

27. b) March 7, 2012

28. c) 73

29. c) 24

30. b) 2014

31. b) November 2014

32. d) Defeat on penalties

33. a) April 2017

34. c) Six

35. b) December 2020

36. b) Winning his first major international trophy

37. b) 2021

38. c) 30

39. b) Seven

40. c) Finalissima

41. c) 26

42. c) Major League Soccer (MLS)

43. c) As children in Rosario

44. c) 2017

45. c) Three

46. c) Barcelona

47. b) Healthcare initiatives for children

48. c) Disaster relief and healthcare

49. b) Sportswear and technology

50. c) Scoring in the penalty shootout

51. c) A clothing and apparel brand

52. c) Bellavista del Jardín del Norte

53. c) Emphasis on exclusivity and elegance

54. c) Joan Miró

55. b) 17

56. b) Abstract and playful pieces

57. c) A distinctive furniture line

58. b) 57

59. b) 12 minutes

60. c) 65

61. d) Every minute, from the first to the last

62. b) 5 feet 7 inches (1.70 meters)

63. b) 23

64. c) 75

65. c) 77

66. a) Left and right fields

67. b) 385

68. b) 24

69. b) 205

70. c) Personal and professional moments

71. b) He maintains a private life

72. c) Exceptional agility and quick changes in direction

73. b) Making crucial passes and setting up goals

74. c) 5

75. d) 13 times

76. b) A solid 25-carat gold cast

77. b) Golden Foot award

78. c) Three

79. b) Arsenal

80. c) Fourth cousins

81. b) Twice

82. d) Second striker

83. c) Playing FIFA on PlayStation

84. b) His grandmother

85. c) Pablo Aimar

86. b) His mother's face

87. b) Enters with his right foot first

88. c) 100 million followers

89. b) Dogue de Bordeaux

90 b) Playing the guitar

91. b) Rapid changes in direction with close ball control

92. c) 12 times

93. c) Hydration and whole foods

94. c) Spanish

95. c) Pilates

96. c) Converted into a fine

97. b) 10

98. b) Introverted personality

99. c) 41

100. c) Agility and quickness

101. d) False nine

5

MESSI QUIZ SCORECARD

Score ___/101

1-20: Beginner Fan

You're just starting to learn about Messi. Keep exploring his story, and your knowledge will surely grow!

21-40: Rising Star

You have a budding understanding of Lionel Messi. Continue your journey, and you'll uncover even more about this football legend!

41-60: In the Game

You're getting to know Messi quite well. Stay curious, and you'll soon be a Messi aficionado!

61-80: Messi Enthusiast

Impressive! You have a solid grasp of Lionel Messi's career and life. Keep up the good work, and you'll soon be a top expert!

81-100: Messi Expert

Fantastic! Your knowledge about Lionel Messi is remarkable. You're nearly at the pinnacle of Messi expertise!

101: Ultimate Messi Fan

Incredible! You've achieved the highest score, proving your status as the ultimate Lionel Messi fan. You truly know him inside and out!

6

RONALDO'S LIFE

Family Roots

On the picturesque island of Madeira, Portugal, a story began that would captivate the world of football. Cristiano Ronaldo dos Santos Aveiro, a name now synonymous with excellence in the sport, was born on February 5, 1985. His early life, set against the backdrop of the serene Madeiran landscape, was marked by humble beginnings and a tightly-knit family unit.

The youngest of four children, Ronaldo was cradled in the nurturing hands of Maria Dolores dos Santos Aveiro and José Dinis Aveiro. Dolores, a hardworking cook, was the pillar of strength and encouragement, fostering young Ronaldo's burgeoning talents. She was the force behind his relentless pursuit of excellence, often accompanying him to training sessions and matches, ensuring that his talents didn't go unnoticed.

José Dinis Aveiro, Ronaldo's father, juggled roles as a municipal gardener and a part-time kit man for Andorinha, the local football club that would be the first to witness Ronaldo's talents. Though his struggles with alcoholism cast a shadow, his influence on Ronaldo's early footballing life was undeniable. Tragically, his battle with alcoholism led to liver failure, resulting in his untimely death in 2005, leaving a void in the young athlete's life.

In the Aveiro household, where the seeds of Ronaldo's future were sown, his older brother Hugo emerged not just as a sibling but as an integral part of the CR7 brand's journey. Hugo's involvement in projects related to Ronaldo's CR7 brand and museum reflects the family's collective pride and contribution to Ronaldo's legacy.

In the Aveiro family, Cristiano wasn't the only one with a flair for the spotlight. His sisters, Elma and Liliana Cátia, carved their own paths. Elma delved into the business world, playing a pivotal role in managing Ronaldo's CR7 fashion brand. Liliana Cátia, also known as Katia Aveiro, channeled her energy into music, becoming a recognized singer in Portugal and releasing several albums. Their diverse talents reflected a family of varied gifts and passions, united in their support for each other.

The name Cristiano Ronaldo, now echoing in stadiums worldwide, has an interesting origin. Named after Ronald Reagan, his father's favorite actor, the choice reflected a fondness for the actor's strength and charisma, qualities that Cristiano would embody in his own life and career.

As a youngster, Ronaldo was affectionately nicknamed 'Cry Baby' and 'Little Bee.' 'Cry Baby' was a nod to his emotional reaction when his passes on the pitch didn't translate into goals, showing his early passion for success and teamwork. 'Little Bee,' on the other hand, was a testament to his remarkable speed, a characteristic that would become a hallmark of his playing style.

Early Beginnings

Ronaldo's journey in football began at the tender age of eight with the amateur team Andorinha in Madeira. His talent was evident even at this young age, setting the stage for a future that would exceed the wildest dreams of the small island club.

Embarking on a transformative journey, Cristiano Ronaldo faced a pivotal moment at the age of 14. The expulsion from school, a consequence of throwing a chair at a teacher in response to perceived disrespect, proved to be a challenging yet defining episode. It marked a turning point in Ronaldo's life, catalyzed by the encouragement of his mother. In the face of adversity, Ronaldo made a decisive choice, redirecting his full attention to soccer. Little did he know that this decision would reshape his destiny, propelling him toward the dazzling heights of global football stardom.

Just a year later, at the age of 15, Ronaldo encountered a critical health challenge—Tachycardia, a condition causing a rapid heartbeat. The potential threat to his career was significant, but Ronaldo faced it head-on. Undergoing a swift and successful heart surgery, employing an advanced laser technique, he emerged from the hospital on the same day with undiminished resolve and physical prowess. This unexpected obstacle, instead of hindering his path, became a crucial stepping stone in Ronaldo's remarkable journey.

At the age of 17, Ronaldo's professional football career took its initial strides as he made his debut for Sporting CP in Portugal. This marked the culmination of a journey that began as a young boy in Madeira and progressed to him emerging as a rising star in Lisbon's Sporting CP. Throughout this trajectory, Ronaldo's character was defined by resilience, passion, and an unwavering determination to excel on the football field.

Rising at Manchester United

In 2003, a new chapter began for Cristiano Ronaldo as his extraordinary talent captured the attention of Manchester United. The English giants secured his signature for a record-breaking £12.24 million ($23.52 million), the highest ever for a teenager at the time, catapulting him into the elite realm of the English Premier League. This monumental move began a transformative era for Ronaldo and the club.

At Manchester United, Ronaldo swiftly became known for his dazzling 'Ronaldo Chop,' a deft step-over move that bewildered defenders and became a signature element of his play. His flair and skill were not just for show; they contributed significantly to the team's success. Ronaldo was instrumental in Manchester United's dominance in the English Premier League, contributing to three consecutive titles in the 2006-07, 2007-08, and 2008-09 seasons. The 2007-08 season was particularly remarkable. Ronaldo's prowess on the field was pivotal in Manchester United clinching the prestigious UEFA Champions League title.

2008 emerged as a defining year in Ronaldo's career. He achieved personal glory by winning his first Ballon d'Or, an accolade affirming his status as the world's best player. That same year, Ronaldo tasted global victory with Manchester United, securing the FIFA Club World Cup.

Real Madrid Era

The year 2009 marked another significant milestone in Ronaldo's career as he made a historic transfer to Real Madrid for a then-world record fee of £80 million. This move shattered transfer records and opened a new chapter of extraordinary achievements in Spain. His nine seasons at Real Madrid were marked by phenomenal success, as he became the club's all-time leading scorer.

Ronaldo's tenure at Real Madrid was laden with silverware, including four impressive Champions League titles. His influence on the pitch was acknowledged globally, earning him the rank of third in the 'World Player of the Decade 2000s,' an accolade placing him among the likes of Lionel Messi and Ronaldinho.

The 2010-11 season saw Ronaldo clinch his first trophy with Real Madrid, winning the Copa del Rey. This victory was not just a triumph for the club but a personal milestone for Ronaldo. In a thrilling final against arch-rivals Barcelona, Ronaldo's spectacular header sealed the win, ending Real Madrid's 18-year drought in the competition and setting a precedent for his future successes with the club.

Continuing his remarkable journey with Real Madrid, Cristiano Ronaldo ushered in the 2011-12 season by clinching his first La Liga title with the club. This achievement was a testament to his relentless pursuit of success and his critical role in driving the team to the pinnacle of Spanish football.

Ronaldo's winning streak continued in the 2012-13 season as he helped Real Madrid secure the Supercopa de España. His relentless drive and exceptional skill on the field were pivotal in conquering this Spanish football championship.

Ronaldo's brilliance was again recognized globally in the 2013-14 season when he was awarded his second Ballon d'Or, symbolizing his stature as one of the best players in the world. That season further cemented his legacy as he led Real Madrid to another Copa del Rey victory and clinched his second Champions League title. Ronaldo set a staggering record in the Champions League, scoring 17 goals in the tournament, a feat unmatched by any player.

In 2014, Ronaldo's trophy cabinet expanded with the addition of his third Ballon d'Or and his second FIFA Club World Cup, both significant acknowledgments of his prowess and contribution to the sport.

2016 marked yet another milestone in Ronaldo's illustrious career. He won his third Champions League with Real Madrid, playing a decisive role in the final against Atlético Madrid by scoring the winning penalty, further elevating his status as a clutch player in high-stakes matches.

The following season was one of unprecedented success for Ronaldo. He won his fourth Ballon d'Or and, after a five-year wait, added another La Liga title to his accolades. He continued his dominance in European football by securing another Champions League trophy and achieved his second Club World Cup, showcasing his extraordinary ability to perform consistently at the highest level.

In the 2017-18 season, his last with Real Madrid, Ronaldo reached new heights by winning his fifth Ballon d'Or in 2017 and clinching his fifth Champions League title. His remarkable performance in the final against Juventus, where he scored twice, was a fitting climax to his time at Real Madrid. Ronaldo set a record as the first player to win the UEFA Champions League five times, a testament to his enduring excellence in European football.

Ronaldo's departure from Real Madrid in July 2018 to join Juventus was a significant moment in football history. He left as Real Madrid's all-time top goal scorer and the only player in La Liga history to score 30 or more goals in six consecutive seasons, a record that speaks volumes of his relentless goal-scoring ability.

From Juventus Back to Manchester United Again

In the summer of 2018, Cristiano Ronaldo made a groundbreaking move to Juventus, with the transfer amounting to a staggering initial £88 million ($100 million). This marked a historic moment, not only as the most expensive transfer for an Italian club but also as the priciest deal involving a player over 30 years old. Ronaldo's arrival at Juventus sparked a period of unparalleled success, contributing significantly to the club's triumphs, including clinching two Serie A titles, securing two Supercoppa Italiana trophies, and lifting the Coppa Italia.

During his tenure with Juventus, Ronaldo left an indelible mark on the Italian football landscape. His exceptional performances were duly recognized when he was bestowed with the inaugural Serie A Most Valuable Player award. Furthermore, Ronaldo etched his name in the annals of football history by becoming the first player ever to secure the top scorer position in the English Premier League, La Liga, and Serie A—underscoring his unparalleled prowess across multiple top-tier leagues.

In a surprising twist, Ronaldo made a highly anticipated return to Manchester United in 2021. In his only full season back at the club, he showcased his enduring goal-scoring prowess by finishing as the top scorer. However, in a turn of events, his contract with Manchester United was terminated in 2022, closing a chapter that had brought moments of triumph and a rekindling of the iconic connection between Ronaldo and the Red Devils.

Debut with Al Nassr

In December 2022, Cristiano signed a two-and-a-half-year contract, estimated by the media to be worth more than 200 million euros ($220.16 million), with the Saudi club Al Nassr. He made his debut there in January 2023, marking a new chapter in his career and demonstrating his continued demand in the football world.

Performance Alongside Portugal

Parallel to his club career, Ronaldo's international journey with Portugal began at 18. He made an immediate impact, scoring his first goal at UEFA Euro 2004 and playing a crucial role in helping Portugal reach the final, signaling the rise of a global football icon on the international stage.

Cristiano Ronaldo's journey on the international stage blossomed in 2006 when he played in his first World Cup, contributing significantly to Portugal's impressive fourth-place finish. His leadership qualities were further recognized in 2008 when he became the full captain of the Portuguese national team. Under his captaincy, Portugal participated in four European Championships (2008, 2012, 2016, 2020) and three FIFA World Cups (2014, 2018, 2022), showcasing his enduring talent and leadership on the global stage.

Skills & Playing Style

Ronaldo's natural right-footedness and exceptional versatility made him an asset in multiple positions on the field. However, he preferred playing as a forward, where he could best utilize his goal-scoring prowess. This positional preference played a significant role in his development into one of football's most prolific scorers.

Furthermore, his physical attributes also set him apart. Celebrated for his lightning speed, he has been recorded reaching speeds of up to 20.9 miles per hour (33.6 kilometers per hour), marking him as one of the fastest players in the sport.

On the pitch, Ronaldo's aerial skills are unparalleled, highlighted by his remarkable record of scoring 145 goals with his head across his tenures at five clubs and the Portugal national team. This ability was vividly showcased in the 2012-13 UEFA Champions League when Ronaldo, playing for Real Madrid, achieved his highest recorded jump of 9 feet 7 inches (2.93m) against Manchester United. Considering his height of 6 feet 2 inches (1.87m), this leap translated to an incredible vertical leap of approximately 41.7 inches (1.06m).

Mastering the art of the 'knuckleball' free kick, Ronaldo has brought an unpredictable element to his game, with 60 free-kick goals. By striking the ball to minimize spin, he created an erratic movement in the air, making it challenging for goalkeepers to predict and defend. His free kicks, often exceeding speeds of 80 miles per hour (130 kilometers per hour), led to some of the most spectacular goals in his career.

Ronaldo has shared the pitch with several notable players on the football field. While at Manchester United, he formed formidable partnerships with Wayne Rooney, Ryan Giggs, and Paul Scholes, contributing to the team's Premier League and Champions League successes. At Real Madrid, he played alongside stars like Sergio Ramos, Luka Modrić, and Karim Benzema. Additionally, his international rivalry with Lionel Messi, representing Portugal and Argentina, respectively, has led to iconic clashes in football history.

Among his numerous memorable goals, one stands out for his sheer audacity and skill. In a Champions League quarter-final match against Juventus, Ronaldo scored a stunning bicycle kick goal, hailed as one of the most spectacular goals in the tournament's history.

Cristiano Ronaldo's career has been marked by numerous records, but one of the most significant is his achievement of 807 career goals, surpassing Josef Bican's long-standing record. This milestone established Ronaldo as the highest-ever goal scorer in the history of men's soccer, a fitting accolade for one of the greatest players the sport has ever seen.

In addition, his precision isn't limited to open play. He has scored 140 penalty kicks in his career, spanning his time at Sporting CP, Manchester United, Real Madrid,

Juventus, and the Portuguese national team. This achievement is a testament to his composure and skill under pressure.

Throughout his career, Ronaldo has continually adapted his playing style. He started as a winger at Manchester United, focusing on delivering crosses. He then transitioned to a more central striker role at Real Madrid, emphasizing goal-scoring. At Juventus, he combined his role as a target man with active dribbling and crossing, showcasing his versatility and commitment to evolving as a player.

Mentorship

Ronaldo's role as a mentor has been instrumental in the development of younger talents. At Manchester United and Real Madrid, he has nurtured players such as Danny Welbeck, Federico Macheda, Lucas Vázquez, and Marco Asensio, boosting their confidence and aiding their growth in top-level football.

In turn, Ronaldo acknowledges the mentors who played a crucial role in his own development, including coaches from Sporting CP and Manchester United. Sir Alex Ferguson, in particular, provided invaluable guidance, and assistant manager Carlos Queiroz was instrumental in shaping Ronaldo into a top-level footballer.

Training, Diet & Mental Fitness

Ronaldo's success is underpinned by a rigorous training regimen. He trains five times a week, with each session lasting 3 to 4 hours and encompassing a mix of cardio exercises, weight training, football drills, and high-intensity interval training. This intense routine is supplemented by core strength exercises, swimming, and Pilates, ensuring his body's balance, recovery, and flexibility.

In addition to physical training, Ronaldo places a strong emphasis on maintaining a meticulously planned diet. Consisting of multiple small meals a day, it focuses on proteins, carbohydrates, and healthy fats. He prioritizes lean meats, whole grains, fresh fruits, and vegetables while steering clear of sugary foods and alcohol.

Beyond the physical and dietary aspects, Ronaldo incorporates mental exercises into his regimen. Meditation and visualization techniques are integral to his routine, enhancing his focus, calmness under pressure, and ability to visualize successful outcomes on the field.

While Ronaldo's career has not been without its challenges, marked by significant injuries such as an ankle injury during the 2008 UEFA European Championship and a knee injury at Real Madrid in 2014, his resilience and determination have seen him swiftly recover and maintain a high-performance level. Despite setbacks like a thigh injury in 2019 and a period of COVID-19 isolation in 2020, Ronaldo's ambition to continue playing at the highest level into his late 30s is a testament to his dedication to maintaining peak physical condition and performance, underscoring his relentless pursuit of excellence in football.

Personal Life & Interests

Cristiano Ronaldo's life significantly changed in 2016 when he met Georgina Rodriguez in Madrid while she was working as a shop assistant at Gucci. Since then, they have built a life together, expanding their family with the arrival of twins Eva and Mateo in 2017 via surrogacy, followed by their daughter Alana Martina later that year.

Family remains at the heart of Ronaldo's life, emphasizing the importance of family values. As a devoted father, he cares for his children, including his firstborn, Cristiano Jr., born in June 2010, over whom he has full custody. Ronaldo dedicates quality time to his children and partner, engaging in simple yet meaningful activities.

His love for travel has taken him and his family to stunning destinations worldwide, from the vibrant nightlife of Ibiza and Miami to the serene beauty of the Maldives and his hometown, Madeira.

An avid animal lover, Ronaldo is fond of dogs, including breeds like bulldogs and labrador retrievers. He often shares his affection for his canine companions on social media, reflecting his softer side and love for animals.

Cristiano Ronaldo's multifaceted personality and career are further highlighted by his proficiency in several languages. His linguistic abilities in English, Spanish, and Italian, in addition to his native Portuguese, have greatly facilitated his international football career. This skill allows him to connect more deeply with fans, teammates, and friends from diverse backgrounds and cultures.

Ronaldo's circle of close friends includes personalities from various fields, reflecting his wide-reaching influence and connections beyond football. These friends include former Manchester United teammates

Patrice Evra and Rio Ferdinand, UFC fighter Conor McGregor, and actor Dwayne 'The Rock' Johnson.

Cristiano Ronaldo's life off the football pitch is as eventful and diverse as his career, encompassing various interests and activities. His involvement in the world of poker extends beyond a mere pastime, as he has participated in professional poker tournaments and promotional events, focusing more on enjoyment and brand promotion than significant monetary gains.

Music also forms an integral part of Ronaldo's life. He is frequently seen at concerts by artists like Rihanna and Jennifer Lopez, sharing his music preferences on social media. His global prominence has led to collaborations with musicians, including appearances in music videos and promotional campaigns, such as those for Ricky Martin.

Each facet of Ronaldo's life, from his career achievements to his personal interests and family values, paints the picture of a multifaceted individual whose impact and legacy extend far beyond the football field.

Fashion & Luxury

Ronaldo's interest in fashion is evident through his active participation in prominent fashion events in cities like Paris and Milan. This involvement showcases not only his prowess on the football field but also his sense of style and engagement with the fashion world.

His hairstyle, a frequent topic of discussion, has become almost as iconic as his football skills. From sleek combed-back looks to edgy spiked designs, Ronaldo's hair has set trends, with the zigzag pattern during the 2014 World Cup standing out. Beyond being a mere fashion statement, his hairstyles are a form of personal expression, widely imitated and extending his influence beyond sports.

In addition to his fashion-forward image, Ronaldo's passion for luxury vehicles is reflected in his impressive collection. This includes exclusive sports cars such as the Bugatti Veyron, Lamborghini Aventador, Ferrari F12, and the standout $3 million Bugatti Chiron. The collection not only showcases his love for high-performance automobiles but also exemplifies his taste for style and the finer things in life.

Complementing his extravagant lifestyle, Ronaldo's ownership of a private jet adds to his ability to manage a hectic schedule. This enables him to balance professional commitments and personal life efficiently, emphasizing his commitment to maintaining a seamless and luxurious lifestyle.

Off the Field Ventures

Cristiano Ronaldo's journey into the world of fragrances marked a unique extension of his brand. In 2017, he introduced 'CR7 Fragrances,' unveiling the 'CR7 Eau de Toilette'—a contemporary, sporty scent mirroring his distinctive style and charisma.

Even before attaining global fame, Ronaldo made an early foray into marketing. In a 2003 television commercial for 'Super Bock,' a Portuguese clothing brand, he showcased one of his initial brand endorsements, providing a glimpse into his early steps in the realm of endorsements.

Ronaldo's worldwide allure is evident in a multitude of brand endorsements. As an ambassador for Clear

Shampoo and Herbalife, he champions hair care and health and wellness products. Simultaneously, he represents TAG Heuer, a prestigious Swiss watch brand, and collaborates with DAZN, a sports streaming service, to boost their sports coverage.

Venturing further into entrepreneurship, Ronaldo has left his mark on the travel industry, associating with American Tourister and co-owning CR7 Hotels in partnership with the Pestana Hotel Group. Additionally, he endorses MTG's healthcare and fitness products, exemplifying his dedication to a lifestyle encompassing health, luxury, and business.

Cristiano Ronaldo's life and career, punctuated by milestones and personal interests, narrate the tale of a man who surpasses the confines of football.

In a monumental move, Ronaldo secured a lifetime endorsement deal with Nike in 2016, valued at a staggering $1 billion. This historic agreement, following in the footsteps of athletes like LeBron James and Michael Jordan, underscores his unparalleled marketing influence. Ronaldo's social media presence alone contributed a remarkable $474 million in value for Nike in 2016, a testament to his immense commercial prowess.

Philanthropy

Cristiano Ronaldo's impact extends beyond the football field through his philanthropic efforts. In 2017, he donated €1.5 million to fund a pediatric hospital in Madeira, his hometown. Recognized as the world's most charitable sportsperson in 2015, he donated €5 million to the earthquake relief efforts in Nepal. His generosity also includes significant contributions to children's charities, funding schools in war zones, and supporting organizations like Save the Children.

In response to the global challenge posed by the COVID-19 pandemic, Ronaldo, alongside his agent Jorge Mendes, stepped up to support hospitals in Portugal. They donated significant funds for critical care beds and medical equipment, playing a crucial role in the fight against the pandemic.

In addition, his commitment to making a difference has seen him involved in campaigns for blood and bone marrow donation. Using his global influence, he raises awareness about these crucial health issues. His personal choice to remain tattoo-free is influenced by his dedication to regularly donating blood, enabling him to avoid the waiting periods often required following tattooing.

Ronaldo's contributions have also had a significant impact on his hometown of Madeira. His donations to local hospitals, the establishment of the CR7 Museum, involvement in youth development programs, and charitable activities through the Cristiano Ronaldo Foundation have positively influenced healthcare, tourism, education, and youth empowerment in the region.

Through his dedication to football, rigorous training, and generous philanthropy, Cristiano Ronaldo has not only etched his name in the annals of sporting history but has also emerged as a role model, demonstrating the impact a global sports icon can have both on and off the field.

Online Presence

Cristiano Ronaldo's dominance in the digital realm is unparalleled. With over 612 million followers, he reigns supreme as the most-followed individual, male figure, sports personality, and European personality on Instagram. His online presence extends beyond Instagram, with a highly-viewed Wikipedia page for a male athlete and a prominent position among the most-followed personalities on Twitter.

What sets Ronaldo apart is not just the numbers but his genuine connection with fans. Known for his accessibility, he readily fulfills requests for selfies and autographs, fostering a personal bond with supporters. His active engagement on social media goes beyond mere postings; he personally responds to comments and messages. This approachable demeanor underscores his deep appreciation for the global fan base that supports him, emphasizing a commitment to reciprocating the admiration he receives.

In the digital landscape, Ronaldo's popularity is not just about statistics; it's a testament to his global influence and the widespread interest he commands. Whether interacting with fans or making waves on various online platforms, Ronaldo's digital footprint showcases a level of engagement and connection that goes beyond traditional notions of sports stardom.

Fun & Random Ronaldo Tidbits

• From a young age, Ronaldo looked up to the Brazilian football legends Ronaldinho and Ronaldo Nazário. He admired their extraordinary skills and the legacy they left in football, often citing them as his idols who inspired him to carve his path in the football world.

• Raised in a devout Catholic family, Ronaldo's faith has been an integral part of his life. While he maintains a private stance on his religious beliefs, his actions, such as making the sign of the cross before games, indicate a deep personal faith.

• Known for his meticulous nature, Ronaldo follows a set of superstitious habits, including stepping onto the pitch with his right foot first and styling his hair before each match. These rituals have become integral to his pre-game routine.

• Upon joining Manchester United in 2003, Ronaldo's limited English necessitated a translator for communication, particularly with Sir Alex Ferguson. Over time, he overcame the language barrier, although he humorously admits to still finding Ferguson's Scottish accent challenging to understand.

• Ronaldo's association with the iconic number 7 jersey at Manchester United has become a significant part of his identity. He inherited this number, which club legends like George Best, Eric Cantona, and David Beckham had worn. He made it synonymous with his legacy.

• In 2009, Real Madrid, recognizing Ronaldo's value, took extraordinary measures to protect their investment; the club insured his legs for a reported sum of around €100 million, underscoring the high esteem in which he was held.

• One of the most iconic elements of Ronaldo's persona is his signature "Siu" celebration, which he debuted in 2013 during a match with Real Madrid against Chelsea.

This dynamic jump, accompanied by a confident shout of "Siu" – meaning "Yes" in Spanish – became synonymous with his moments of triumph and joy upon scoring.

• On the field, Ronaldo's competitive nature has occasionally led to controversy. His intensity and passion have resulted in several red cards and debates over his sportsmanship, particularly his reactions to referee decisions and confrontations with opponents.

• In 2017, Ronaldo faced accusations of tax evasion in Spain, involving €14.7 million related to image rights income. He settled the case in 2019, accepting a suspended jail sentence and agreeing to pay €18.8 million in fines, avoiding jail time.

• In the virtual world of FIFA 18, Ronaldo was recognized as the highest-rated player, with an overall rating of 99%, showcasing his prominence in the sport.

• In 2020, as reported by Forbes, Ronaldo made history as the first active team sport athlete to surpass $1 billion in career earnings.

• The CR7 Museum in Funchal, Madeira, inaugurated in 2013, pays homage to Ronaldo's illustrious career. It houses a collection of his trophies, medals, photographs from his childhood, and memorabilia from significant matches, offering fans a comprehensive look at his journey.

• Ronaldo's fame is reflected in his representation as a waxwork at Madame Tussauds in London, joining football legends like Steven Gerrard, Pelé, and David Beckham. This honor celebrates his achievements and popularity in the realm of sports.

7

TRIVIA QUESTIONS

1. What is Cristiano Ronaldo's full name and where was he born?

a) Cristiano Ronaldo de Silva, Lisbon, Portugal

b) Cristiano Ronaldo dos Santos Aveiro, Madeira, Portugal

c) Cristiano Ronaldo Fernandes, Porto, Portugal

d) Cristiano Ronaldo Soares, Faro, Portugal

2. Cristiano Ronaldo is the youngest child of how many siblings?

a) Two

b) Three

c) Four

d) Five

3. What was Cristiano Ronaldo's father's profession?

a) Teacher

b) Football coach

c) Municipal gardener and part-time kit man

d) Mechanic

4. What role did Ronaldo's mother play in his early football career?

a) She was his first coach

b) She managed his early contracts

c) She encouraged his talent and took him to training sessions

d) She funded his football academy fees

5. What is Ronaldo's older brother, Hugo, known for?

a) Being a professional footballer

b) Working on Ronaldo's CR7 brand and museum

c) Managing Ronaldo's finances

d) Coaching in the youth academy

6. What are Cristiano Ronaldo's sisters' names and professions?

a) Elma (fashion designer) and Liliana Cátia (lawyer)

b) Elma (manages CR7 fashion brand) and Liliana Cátia (singer)

c) Elma (teacher) and Liliana Cátia (architect)

d) Elma (businesswoman) and Liliana Cátia (chef)

7. After whom was Cristiano Ronaldo named?

a) Ronaldinho, a footballer

b) Ronald Reagan, an actor

c) Ronaldo Nazário, a footballer

d) Ronald McDonald, a fictional character

8. What were Ronaldo's childhood nicknames?

a) 'Speedy' and 'Goal Machine'

b) 'Cristy' and 'Rocket'

c) 'Cry Baby' and 'Little Bee'

d) 'Junior' and 'Flash'

9. At what age did Cristiano Ronaldo start playing football and for which team?

a) 6, Porto

b) 8, Andorinha

c) 10, Sporting CP

d) 12, Benfica

10. Why was Cristiano Ronaldo expelled from school at age 14?

a) Poor grades

b) Fighting with classmates

c) Throwing a chair at his teacher

d) Skipping classes to play football

11. What medical condition did Cristiano Ronaldo have at the age of 15, requiring heart surgery?

a) Arrhythmia

b) Tachycardia

c) Hypertension

d) Cardiomyopathy

12. When did Cristiano Ronaldo begin his professional football career?

a) 2000

b) 2001

c) 2002

d) 2003

13. Which club signed Cristiano Ronaldo in 2003, for a then-record fee for a teenager?

a) Barcelona

b) Manchester United

c) Real Madrid

d) AC Milan

14. What signature move is Cristiano Ronaldo known for during his time at Manchester United?

a) The Ronaldo Turn

b) The Ronaldo Chop

c) The Ronaldo Spin

d) The Ronaldo Dash

15. How many consecutive Premier League titles did Ronaldo win with Manchester United?

a) One

b) Two

c) Three

d) Four

16. In which season did Ronaldo help Manchester United win the UEFA Champions League?

a) 2005-06

b) 2006-07

c) 2007-08

d) 2008-09

17. When did Ronaldo win his first FIFA Club World Cup with Manchester United?

a) 2006

b) 2007

c) 2008

d) 2009

18. In which year did Cristiano Ronaldo win his first Ballon d'Or?

a) 2006

b) 2007

c) 2008

d) 2009

19. For how much was Cristiano Ronaldo transferred to Real Madrid in 2009, setting a world record at the time?

a) £60 million

b) £70 million

c) £80 million

d) £90 million

20. How many seasons did Ronaldo spend at Real Madrid, becoming the club's all-time leading scorer?

a) Seven

b) Eight

c) Nine

d) Ten

21. How many Champions League titles did Cristiano Ronaldo win during his time at Real Madrid?

a) Two

b) Three

c) Four

d) Five

22. Where was Ronaldo ranked in the 'World Player of the Decade 2000s'?

a) First

b) Second

c) Third

d) Fourth

23. In which season did Ronaldo win his first trophy with Real Madrid?

a) 2009-10

b) 2010-11

c) 2011-12

d) 2012-13

24. Which title did Ronaldo secure with Real Madrid in the 2011-12 season?

a) Champions League

b) La Liga

c) Copa del Rey

d) Supercopa de España

25. What did Ronaldo win with Real Madrid in the 2012-13 season?

a) Champions League

b) La Liga

c) Copa del Rey

d) Supercopa de España

26. In which season did Ronaldo win his second Ballon d'Or?

a) 2011-12

b) 2012-13

c) 2013-14

d) 2014-15

27. How many goals did Ronaldo score in the Champions League in the 2013-14 season, setting a record?

a) 15

b) 16

c) 17

d) 18

28. What did Ronaldo win in 2014, along with his third Ballon d'Or?

a) La Liga

b) Copa del Rey

c) Champions League

d) FIFA Club World Cup

29. In which year did Ronaldo win his third Champions League with Real Madrid, scoring the winning penalty in the final?

a) 2014

b) 2015

c) 2016

d) 2017

30. What achievements did Ronaldo earn in the season following his third Champions League win with Real Madrid?

a) Fourth Ballon d'Or, La Liga title, Champions League, Club World Cup

b) Third Ballon d'Or, Copa del Rey, Supercopa de España

c) Fifth Ballon d'Or, La Liga title, Europa League

d) Fourth Ballon d'Or, Copa del Rey, Champions League

31. What were the major achievements of Ronaldo's last season with Real Madrid in 2017-18?

a) Fifth Ballon d'Or and fourth Champions League title

b) Fourth Ballon d'Or and fifth Champions League title

c) Fifth Ballon d'Or and fifth Champions League title

d) Sixth Ballon d'Or and fifth Champions League title

32. Ronaldo set a record as the first player to win how many UEFA Champions League titles?

a) Three

b) Four

c) Five

d) Six

33. When Ronaldo transferred to Juventus in 2018, what record did he leave behind at Real Madrid?

a) All-time top goal scorer with 30 or more goals in five consecutive seasons

b) All-time top goal scorer with 40 or more goals in six consecutive seasons

c) All-time top goal scorer with 30 or more goals in six consecutive seasons

d) All-time top goal scorer with 50 or more goals in four consecutive seasons

34. At what age did Ronaldo begin his international career with Portugal, and when did he score his first goal?

a) 16 years old, UEFA Euro 2004

b) 18 years old, UEFA Euro 2004

c) 20 years old, FIFA World Cup 2006

d) 18 years old, FIFA World Cup 2006

35. In which year did Ronaldo play in his first World Cup, and what was Portugal's finish?

a) 2004, semi-finals

b) 2006, fourth place

c) 2008, quarter-finals

d) 2010, round of 16

36. Since what year has Ronaldo been the full captain of Portugal, and in how many European Championships and FIFA World Cups has he participated since then?

a) 2008, four European Championships and three FIFA World Cups

b) 2006, three European Championships and four FIFA World Cups

c) 2010, four European Championships and four FIFA World Cups

d) 2004, five European Championships and three FIFA World Cups

37. Which Brazilian football legends did Ronaldo admire during his youth?

a) Pele and Zico

b) Ronaldinho and Ronaldo Nazário

c) Rivaldo and Romário

d) Cafu and Roberto Carlos

38. What is Ronaldo's preferred position on the field?

a) Winger

b) Forward

c) Midfielder

d) Defender

39. What is Ronaldo's recorded top speed on the pitch?

a) 17.9 miles per hour

b) 19.2 miles per hour

c) 20.9 miles per hour

d) 22.4 miles per hour

40. How tall is Cristiano Ronaldo and what is his vertical leap?

a) 6 feet, 28.7 inches

b) 6 feet 1 inch, 30.7 inches

c) 6 feet 2 inches, 32.7 inches

d) 6 feet 2 inches, 41.7 inches

41. What is the name of the free kick technique mastered by Ronaldo, which involves minimizing spin on the ball?

a) The Rocket Kick

b) The Curveball Kick

c) The Knuckleball Free Kick

d) The Spinball Kick

42. How many penalty kicks has Ronaldo scored in his professional club and international career?

a) 100

b) 120

c) 140

d) 160

43. How many hat-tricks has Ronaldo scored in his professional career for club and country?

a) 40

b) 50

c) 60

d) 70

44. What does Cristiano Ronaldo's signature "Siu" celebration mean in Spanish?

a) Jump

b) Victory

c) Yes

d) Amazing

45. As of the given facts, how many career goals has Cristiano Ronaldo achieved, surpassing Josef Bican's record?

a) 785

b) 795

c) 807

d) 815

46. How many goals has Ronaldo scored with his head across his tenures at five clubs and the Portugal national team?

a) 125

b) 135

c) 145

d) 155

47. What is Ronaldo's highest recorded jump height, achieved in the UEFA Champions League against Manchester United?

a) 8 feet 9 inches

b) 9 feet 7 inches

c) 10 feet 2 inches

d) 10 feet 6 inches

48. Against which team did Ronaldo score a celebrated bicycle kick goal in a Champions League quarter-final match?

a) Barcelona

b) Juventus

c) Bayern Munich

d) Paris Saint-Germain

49. What was the reported sum for which Real Madrid insured Ronaldo's legs in 2009?

a) Around €50 million

b) Around €75 million

c) Around €100 million

d) Around €125 million

50. How long does each of Ronaldo's training sessions typically last?

a) 1 to 2 hours

b) 2 to 3 hours

c) 3 to 4 hours

d) 4 to 5 hours

51. What additional exercises does Ronaldo incorporate into his training regimen for balance, recovery, and flexibility?

a) Yoga, Running, and Weightlifting

b) Core Strength Exercises, Swimming, and Pilates

c) Boxing, Cycling, and Aerobics

d) Martial Arts, Dance, and Sprinting

52. How is Cristiano Ronaldo's diet planned?

a) High in protein, low in carbs, no fruits or vegetables

b) Multiple small meals a day, rich in protein, carbohydrates, and healthy fats

c) One large meal a day, low in fats, high in protein

d) Vegetarian diet, excluding all forms of meat

53. What mental exercises does Ronaldo include in his training regimen?

a) Hypnosis and Deep Breathing

b) Meditation and Visualization Techniques

c) Cognitive Behavioral Therapy and Positive Affirmations

d) Neuro-Linguistic Programming and Mindfulness

54. How much did Ronaldo donate to fund a pediatric hospital in Madeira in 2017?

a) €500,000

b) €1 million

c) €1.5 million

d) €2 million

55. In which year was Ronaldo named the world's most charitable sportsperson?

a) 2012

b) 2015

c) 2018

d) 2020

56. Which children's charity does Ronaldo frequently contribute to?

a) UNICEF

b) Save the Children

c) World Vision

d) Plan International

57. What campaigns has Ronaldo been involved in to raise awareness?

a) Cancer research and mental health

b) Blood donation and bone marrow donation

c) Climate change and environmental protection

d) Animal rights and veganism

58. Why has Cristiano Ronaldo chosen not to have any tattoos?

a) Personal preference

b) Religious beliefs

c) Commitment to regularly donating blood

d) Allergic to tattoo ink

59. What did Ronaldo and his agent Jorge Mendes donate during the COVID-19 pandemic?

a) Funds for vaccines and research

b) Funds for critical care beds and medical equipment

c) Food and supplies for those affected

d) Personal protective equipment for healthcare workers

60. What religious gesture does Ronaldo often make before games?

a) Making the cross sign

b) Kneeling and praying

c) Bowing towards Mecca

d) Meditating silently

61. What is the name of Cristiano Ronaldo's signature fragrance line, launched in 2017?

a) CR7 Elegance

b) CR7 Fragrances

c) Ronaldo Essence

d) Cristiano Scents

62. In which year did Ronaldo appear in a television commercial for 'Super Bock,' marking one of his earliest brand endorsements?

a) 2001

b) 2003

c) 2005

d) 2007

63. How much in image rights income was Ronaldo accused of evading in taxes by Spanish authorities in 2017?

a) €10.7 million

b) €12.7 million

c) €14.7 million

d) €16.7 million

64. Ronaldo's competitive nature on the field has led to several red cards and criticism. What aspects of his behavior have been debated?

a) Goal celebrations and interviews

b) Reactions to referee decisions and confrontations with opponents

c) Team selection and coaching criticism

d) Media interactions and sponsorship deals

65. Which brands does Ronaldo represent as a global ambassador?

a) Adidas and Gatorade

b) Clear Shampoo and Herbalife

c) Puma and Red Bull

d) Under Armour and Monster Energy

66. Which high-end Swiss watch brand and sports streaming service does Ronaldo represent?

a) Rolex and ESPN

b) TAG Heuer and DAZN

c) Omega and Sky Sports

d) Breitling and Hulu Sports

67. In addition to his football career, Ronaldo has business ventures in various industries. Which of these does he not have a collaboration with?

a) American Tourister

b) CR7 Hotels with the Pestana Hotel Group

c) MTG's healthcare and fitness products

d) A personal airline company

68. Which World Cup saw Ronaldo sporting a zigzag hairstyle, becoming a trend among fans?

a) 2010 World Cup

b) 2014 World Cup

c) 2018 World Cup

d) 2022 World Cup

69. Which of these luxury cars is not in Cristiano Ronaldo's collection?

a) Bugatti Veyron

b) Lamborghini Aventador

c) Ferrari F12

d) McLaren P1

70. Since when has Cristiano Ronaldo been under a lifetime endorsement deal with Nike, and how much is it valued at?

a) Since 2014, valued at $500 million

b) Since 2016, valued at $1 billion

c) Since 2018, valued at $750 million

d) Since 2020, valued at $1.5 billion

71. What is the purpose of Ronaldo's private jet?

a) To attend charity events only

b) To travel for professional football matches and personal commitments

c) To participate in air races

d) For luxury tourism business

72. When was the CR7 Museum in Funchal, Madeira, inaugurated, and what does it showcase?

a) 2010, showcasing his luxury car collection

b) 2013, showcasing his career achievements and personal life

c) 2015, showcasing his fashion and fragrance lines

d) 2018, showcasing his real estate investments

73. How many free-kick goals has Ronaldo scored in his professional career?

a) 40

b) 50

c) 60

d) 70

74. When did Cristiano Ronaldo's relationship with Georgina Rodriguez begin?

a) 2014

b) 2015

c) 2016

d) 2017

75. How many children does Cristiano Ronaldo have, and how was his second set of children born?

a) Three, via surrogacy

b) Four, with two born via surrogacy

c) Five, with one adopted

d) Four, all naturally born

76. What does Cristiano Ronaldo emphasize as an important aspect of his life?

a) His car collection

b) Fashion and style

c) Family values

d) His football legacy

77. What milestone did Ronaldo achieve in 2020 in terms of career earnings?

a) $500 million

b) $750 million

c) $1 billion

d) $1.5 billion

78. Which of the following is not listed as one of Ronaldo's favorite vacation spots?

a) Ibiza

b) Miami

c) Tokyo

d) Maldives

79. Which fashion events does Ronaldo actively participate in?

a) New York and London Fashion Weeks

b) Paris and Milan Fashion Weeks

c) Berlin and Sydney Fashion Weeks

d) Toronto and São Paulo Fashion Weeks

80. When did Cristiano Ronaldo make his debut for Al Nassr?

a) December 2022

b) January 2023

c) February 2023

d) March 2023

81. What is Ronaldo's involvement in professional poker tournaments?

a) Primarily for significant monetary gains

b) Mainly for enjoyment and brand promotion

c) As a professional poker player

d) For charity fundraising events

82. Which musicians have Ronaldo collaborated with, as reflected in his appearances in music videos and promotional campaigns?

a) Beyoncé and Jay-Z

b) Ricky Martin and Shakira

c) Ricky Martin and Jennifer Lopez

d) Ed Sheeran and Taylor Swift

83. Which notable players did Ronaldo share the pitch with during his time at Manchester United?

a) David Beckham, Ryan Giggs, and Paul Scholes

b) Wayne Rooney, Ryan Giggs, and Paul Scholes

c) Nemanja Vidić, Rio Ferdinand, and Wayne Rooney

d) Gary Neville, David Beckham, and Roy Keane

84. Who were Ronaldo's teammates at Real Madrid, contributing to the team's success?

a) Gareth Bale, Karim Benzema, and James Rodríguez

b) Sergio Ramos, Luka Modrić, and Karim Benzema

c) Iker Casillas, Marcelo, and Toni Kroos

d) Isco, Raphael Varane, and Keylor Navas

85. What is the estimated value of Ronaldo's contract with Al Nassr, signed in 2023?

a) More than 150 million euros

b) More than 200 million euros

c) More than 250 million euros

d) More than 300 million euros

86. Which significant injuries has Ronaldo faced throughout his career?

a) Ankle, knee, thigh injuries, and COVID-19 isolation

b) Shoulder, back, hamstring injuries, and flu

c) Concussion, wrist, hip injuries, and malaria

d) Elbow, shin, calf injuries, and chickenpox

87. In the digital realm, what distinguishes Cristiano Ronaldo's Wikipedia page?

a) Most-edited page

b) Most-viewed page for a male athlete

c) Longest page in terms of content

d) Highest-rated page by users

88. Who are some of the young talents Ronaldo has mentored at Manchester United and Real Madrid?

a) Danny Welbeck, Federico Macheda, Lucas Vázquez, Marco Asensio

b) Jesse Lingard, Marcus Rashford, Álvaro Morata, Isco

c) Adnan Januzaj, Ángel Di María, Casemiro, Nacho

d) Javier Hernández, Mateo Kovačić, Dani Carvajal, Jesé

89. Which famous personalities are among Cristiano Ronaldo's close friends?

a) Lionel Messi, Neymar Jr., and LeBron James

b) Patrice Evra, Rio Ferdinand, Conor McGregor, Dwayne 'The Rock' Johnson

c) David Beckham, Cristiano Jr., and Khabib Nurmagomedov

d) Paul Pogba, Marcelo, and Kevin Hart

90. How is Ronaldo known to interact with fans?

a) Rarely interacts or grants requests for selfies and autographs

b) Often grants requests for selfies and autographs

c) Only interacts with fans at official events

d) Primarily interacts through his management team

91. In addition to Portuguese, what other languages is Cristiano Ronaldo proficient in?

a) German, French, and Russian

b) English, Spanish, and Italian

c) Dutch, Japanese, and Arabic

d) Swedish, Chinese, and Greek

92. How has Ronaldo impacted his hometown of Madeira, Portugal?

a) By building a sports complex and a university

b) Through donations, the CR7 Museum, and youth programs

c) By establishing a football academy and a theme park

d) Through real estate development and creating job opportunities

93. What type of animals is Ronaldo known to be an avid lover of?

a) Cats

b) Horses

c) Dogs

d) Birds

94. Who were Ronaldo's early mentors?

a) Pep Guardiola and Zinedine Zidane

b) José Mourinho and Carlo Ancelotti

c) Sir Alex Ferguson and Carlos Queiroz

d) Arsène Wenger and Frank Rijkaard

95. What was Ronaldo's overall rating in FIFA 18, making him the highest-rated player?

a) 97%

b) 98%

c) 99%

d) 100%

96. Which iconic jersey number is associated with Cristiano Ronaldo at Manchester United?

a) Number 7

b) Number 10

c) Number 11

d) Number 9

97. What type of superstitious habits is Ronaldo known for?

a) Wearing the same socks for every match

b) Stepping onto the pitch with his right foot first

c) Always playing with a wristband

d) Listening to the same song before every match

98. Upon joining Manchester United, what language barrier did Ronaldo face?

a) Difficulty in understanding Spanish

b) Limited grasp of English

c) Inability to speak French

d) Challenges with Italian

99. Cristiano Ronaldo became the fourth footballer to have what honor at Madame Tussauds in London?

a) A documentary film

b) A waxwork

c) A bronze statue

d) An exclusive gallery

100. What record does Ronaldo hold on Instagram?

a) Most-followed athlete

b) Most-followed European personality

c) Both of the above

d) Most likes on a single post

101. How has Ronaldo's playing style evolved throughout his career?

a) From a striker to a winger

b) From a midfielder to a forward

c) From a winger to a central striker

d) From a defender to a midfielder

8

TRIVIA ANSWERS

1. b) Cristiano Ronaldo dos Santos Aveiro, Madeira, Portugal

2. c) Four

3. c) Municipal gardener and part-time kit man

4. c) She encouraged his talent and took him to training sessions

5. b) Working on Ronaldo's CR7 brand and museum

6. b) Elma (manages CR7 fashion brand) and Liliana Cátia (singer)

7. b) Ronald Reagan, an actor

8. c) 'Cry Baby' and 'Little Bee'

9. b) 8, Andorinha

10. c) Throwing a chair at his teacher

11. b) Tachycardia

12. c) 2002

13. b) Manchester United

14. b) The Ronaldo Chop

15. c) Three

16. c) 2007-08

17. c) 2008

18. c) 2008

19. c) £80 million

20. c) Nine

21. c) Four

22. c) Third

23. b) 2010-11

24. b) La Liga

25. d) Supercopa de España

26. c) 2013-14

27. c) 17

28. d) FIFA Club World Cup

29. c) 2016

30. a) Fourth Ballon d'Or, La Liga title, Champions League, Club World Cup

31. c) Fifth Ballon d'Or and fifth Champions League title

32. c) Five

33. c) All-time top goal scorer with 30 or more goals in six consecutive seasons

34. b) 18 years old, UEFA Euro 2004

35. b) 2006, fourth place

36. a) 2008, four European Championships and three FIFA World Cups

37. b) Ronaldinho and Ronaldo Nazário

38. b) Forward

39. c) 20.9 miles per hour

40. d) 6 feet 2 inches, 41.7 inches

41. c) The Knuckleball Free Kick

42. c) 140

43. c) 60

44. c) Yes

45. c) 807

46. c) 145

47. b) 9 feet 7 inches

48. b) Juventus

49. c) Around €100 million

50. c) 3 to 4 hours

51. b) Core Strength Exercises, Swimming, and Pilates

52. b) Multiple small meals a day, rich in protein, carbohydrates, and healthy fats

53. b) Meditation and Visualization Techniques

54. c) €1.5 million

55. b) 2015

56. b) Save the Children

57. b) Blood donation and bone marrow donation

58. c) Commitment to regularly donating blood

59. b) Funds for critical care beds and medical equipment

60. a) Making the cross sign

61. b) CR7 Fragrances

62. b) 2003

63. c) €14.7 million

64. b) Reactions to referee decisions and confrontations with opponents

65. b) Clear Shampoo and Herbalife

66. b) TAG Heuer and DAZN

67. d) A personal airline company

68. b) 2014 World Cup

69. d) McLaren P1

70. b) Since 2016, valued at $1 billion

71. b) To travel for professional football matches and personal commitments

72. b) 2013, showcasing his career achievements and personal life

73. c) 60

74. c) 2016

75. b) Four, with two born via surrogacy

76. c) Family values

77. c) $1 billion

78. c) Tokyo

79. b) Paris and Milan Fashion Weeks

80. b) January 2023

81. b) Mainly for enjoyment and brand promotion

82. c) Ricky Martin and Jennifer Lopez

83. b) Wayne Rooney, Ryan Giggs, and Paul Scholes

84. b) Sergio Ramos, Luka Modrić, and Karim Benzema

85. b) More than 200 million euros

86. a) Ankle, knee, thigh injuries, and COVID-19 isolation

87. b) Most-viewed page for a male athlete

88. a) Danny Welbeck, Federico Macheda, Lucas Vázquez, Marco Asensio

89. b) Patrice Evra, Rio Ferdinand, Conor McGregor, Dwayne 'The Rock' Johnson

90. b) Often grants requests for selfies and autographs

91. b) English, Spanish, and Italian

92. b) Through donations, the CR7 Museum, and youth programs

93. c) Dogs

94. c) Sir Alex Ferguson and Carlos Queiroz

95. c) 99%

96. a) Number 7

97. b) Stepping onto the pitch with his right foot first

98. b) Limited grasp of English

99. b) A waxwork

100. c) Both of the above

101. c) From a winger to a central striker

9

RONALDO QUIZ SCORECARD

Score ___/101

1-20: Beginner Fan

You're just starting to learn about Ronaldo. Keep exploring his story, and your knowledge will surely grow!

21-40: Rising Star

You have a budding understanding of Cristiano Ronaldo. Continue your journey, and you'll uncover even more about this football legend!

41-60: In the Game

You're getting to know Ronaldo quite well. Stay curious, and you'll soon be a Ronaldo aficionado!

61-80: Ronaldo Enthusiast

Impressive! You have a solid grasp of Cristiano Ronaldo's career and life. Keep up the good work, and you'll soon be a top expert!

81-100: Ronaldo Expert

Fantastic! Your knowledge about Cristiano Ronaldo is remarkable. You're nearly at the pinnacle of Ronaldo expertise!

101: Ultimate Ronaldo Fan

Incredible! You've achieved the highest score, proving your status as the ultimate Cristiano Ronaldo fan. You truly know CR7 inside and out!

10

SO, WHO'S THE BEST?

The Ultimate Showdown! Who reigns supreme? In one corner, we have the magical Lionel Messi, and in the other, the powerhouse Cristiano Ronaldo. These soccer legends have not only defined an era but have also sparked endless debates in cafes, living rooms, and stadiums worldwide. With careers that have mirrored each other in brilliance and longevity, they've been the twin titans of the turf, each dazzling us with their unique brand of footballing genius. We're diving into a fun-filled, stats-packed comparison across various categories. Who will emerge as the ultimate football maestro?

11

MESSI VS. RONALDO

Goal Galore

In the thrilling goal-scoring face-off, Messi and Ronaldo have truly set the football world alight. Imagine this: at their peak, these legends were bagging goals as if they were going out of style, averaging more than one per game!

Rewind to Ronaldo's spellbinding nine years at Real Madrid, where both titans scored a goal every 85 minutes, turning goal-scoring into an art form.

Zooming out to their overall careers, Messi sneaks ahead with a sharp 0.78 goals per game, while Ronaldo is hot on his heels with 0.72. Breaking it down to minutes, Messi finds the net every 105 minutes, with Ronaldo making his mark every 112 minutes.

But here's the kicker: Ronaldo boasts a higher total with 869 career goals against Messi's 821, though he's played 154 more matches.

Ronaldo's journey from a traditional winger to a goal-scoring juggernaut took about 3-4 years, whereas Messi transformed from a speedy winger into a goal-centric force in 2-3 years. Factor in these early roles, and their goal ratios draw even closer.

In this goal-scoring race, picking a winner is as tough as it gets, with both champions matching each other stride for stride in their quest for the back of the net!

Dishing it Out

In the realm of setting up goals, one maestro takes the crown. Lionel Messi, the masterful playmaker, has an astonishing record to back his top-tier status in the assist department.

Messi's magic has led to a staggering 361 assists in 1047 appearances, a testament to his visionary play. Ronaldo, not far behind in the creative game, has a respectable tally of 248 assists across 1201 matches.

But here's a twist: despite Messi's dominance in assist numbers, it's easy to overlook Ronaldo's prowess as a playmaker. His assist stats, especially when compared to the mere mortals of football, are nothing short of impressive.

Diving into the Champions League, Ronaldo even edges past Messi, notching up 41 assists to Messi's 40, albeit in 20 more games. This achievement adds a sparkle to Ronaldo's already brilliant assisting record.

Despite Ronaldo's commendable showing in Europe's premier club competition, Messi's overall assist figures are too monumental to be overshadowed. In the art of the assist, Messi leads, weaving his magic with every pass!

Pass Masters

When it comes to threading the needle with precision passes, the stats make a strong case for a leader, and it's Lionel Messi. However, let's not rush to overlook Cristiano Ronaldo's underappreciated passing skills.

Since the 2009/10 season, both in domestic leagues and the Champions League, Messi has been a passing prodigy, delivering 1393 key passes in 599 appearances. Ronaldo, with his own brand of playmaking, has crafted 940 key passes in 561 games – impressive in its own right.

Messi shines even brighter in the throughball game, masterfully executing 450 successful throughballs in the same period, dwarfing Ronaldo's commendable 81.

While Messi's numbers are undeniably superior, painting him as the pass master supreme, Ronaldo's stats are still noteworthy. It's worth pondering that Ronaldo's passing contributions might have been even more substantial before 2009, during his more creatively involved days.

In the realm of passing, Messi may lead the pack, but Ronaldo's abilities are far from ordinary, showcasing his versatility on the field.

Dribbling Wizards

The art of dribbling has always been a dazzling aspect of football, and in this arena, both Messi and Ronaldo have had their moments of magic. Ronaldo began as a fleet-footed winger, known for his electrifying runs and skills to outpace defenders. Yet, as he evolved into a lethal inside-forward/striker, his reliance on dribbling took a backseat to other aspects of his game.

Messi, on the other hand, also kicked off his career hugging the sidelines. But unlike Ronaldo, he shifted to a more central role, becoming a unique blend of a traditional Number 10 and a False 9. This position change meant Messi often dropped deeper into the play, rather than waiting on the last defender's shoulder.

This deeper involvement is where Messi's dribbling prowess truly shines. He has weaved his way through defenses with an astounding 3202 successful dribbles in league and Champions League play, a stark contrast to Ronaldo's impressive but lesser 1687 since 2003/04.

In the dance of dribbling, Messi undeniably takes the spotlight, with his close control and ability to glide past opponents being second to none. Ronaldo's early days showcased his dribbling skills, but Messi's consistent application of this art throughout his career crowns him the king of dribbling finesse.

Aerial Acrobats

When the ball takes to the air, there's a clear champion in the heading game between Messi and Ronaldo. Ronaldo, with his formidable aerial ability, dominates this category by a significant margin.

Throughout their careers, Ronaldo has been a towering presence, netting an astonishing 146 headers in 1201 appearances. Messi, with a more grounded style of play, has notched up 26 headers in 1047 appearances. The difference isn't just stark; it's colossal.

But it's not just about scoring with his head; Ronaldo's mastery extends to winning aerial duels too. Since the 2009/10 season, he has soared above his competitors to win 779 aerial battles in league and Champions League matches, overshadowing Messi's 116.

This disparity in their heading prowess is hardly a shock when you consider their physical attributes, playing styles, and how their teams utilize their unique strengths. Ronaldo, with his athletic build and leap, is a natural in the air, while Messi, known for his close-to-the-ground brilliance, focuses on weaving magic with his feet.

In the realm of aerial challenges and headed goals, Ronaldo is the undisputed king, ruling the skies with his head.

Sharpshooters in Focus

When it comes to taking aim and firing shots on goal, Messi and Ronaldo present a fascinating study in contrasts. Ronaldo, the relentless shooter, has unleashed a staggering 3668 shots in league and Champions League play since 2009/10. Messi, not far behind, has made 2941 attempts in the same period.

But here's where the plot thickens: Messi is the sniper, boasting a higher shot conversion rate. He scores with every 5.27 attempts, demonstrating remarkable efficiency. Ronaldo, on the other hand, finds the back of the net every 6.43 shots.

Accuracy? Messi shines here too, with a solid 47.19% of his shots hitting the target, outperforming Ronaldo's 41.19%.

However, the tale doesn't end there. Ronaldo's sheer ability to generate a high volume of shots is a testament to his enduring threat and persistence. He's not just a shooter; he's a siege engine, firing from all ranges, with both feet, and his head. This relentless shooting strategy, coupled with his prowess in long-range efforts and versatility, levels the playing field.

In the realm of shooting, it's a thrilling draw. Messi wows with his precision and efficiency, while Ronaldo impresses with his voluminous and varied shooting arsenal. Both styles are different, yet equally mesmerizing.

Penalty Showdown

In the high-stakes world of penalty kicks, a realm where nerves of steel and precision are key, Ronaldo emerges with a noticeable edge over Messi. However, the gap might not be as wide as popular belief suggests.

Ronaldo, often hailed as the unflappable penalty maestro, has racked up 158 successful penalties from the spot, missing 29 across his career. Messi, sometimes unfairly tagged as less reliable, has scored 108 penalties with 31 misses. This puts Ronaldo at an impressive 84% conversion rate, slightly outshining Messi's respectable 78%.

While Ronaldo's numbers are superior, it's worth noting that he isn't infallible. Other top strikers like

Lewandowski and Ibrahimovic have shown even higher rates of consistency from the penalty spot.

High-pressure misses? Both legends have had their moments. Messi's notable misses include the 2016 Copa America final against Chile and the 2012 Champions League semi-final against Chelsea. Ronaldo, too, has faced his share of crucial misses, like in the 2008 Champions League final against Chelsea and the 2012 semi-final against Bayern Munich.

In the penalty box face-off, Ronaldo holds the statistical upper hand, but the narrative of Messi being a weak link from the spot doesn't quite hold up under scrutiny. Both have shown remarkable prowess, with Ronaldo just a step ahead in this specific skill set.

Free Kick Finesse

The battle of free kicks between Messi and Ronaldo is a tale of evolving mastery and shifting tides. In recent times, Messi has ascended to become a free kick wizard, while Ronaldo's magic in this domain has seen a surprising dip.

It's a game of two halves: between 2017 and 2019, Messi bent the ball into the net an astonishing 23 times from free kicks, dwarfing Ronaldo's 5 during the same period. However, roll back the clock to 2009-2011, and it was Ronaldo who was the free kick king, scoring 21 to Messi's 3.

Looking at their career-long achievements paints an intriguing picture. Messi has curled in a total of 65 free kick goals, just nudging ahead of Ronaldo's 61. This shift in free kick prowess is a stark contrast to a few years back when Ronaldo seemed the undisputed lord of the set-piece.

What we're witnessing is Messi's remarkable catch-up and eventual overtaking in this category, now boasting a superior conversion rate. Once a realm dominated by Ronaldo, the free kick battleground has seen a changing of the guard, with Messi now edging it with his recent spellbinding performances.

Hat Trick Heroes

When it comes to hat tricks, Messi and Ronaldo are in a league of their own, collectively amassing a mind-blowing 120 between them. Ronaldo, with a total of 63 career hat tricks, has a slim numerical lead over Messi's 57. But the plot thickens when we look at the frequency of these scoring feats.

Messi, the maestro of multi-goal matches, nets a hat trick every 18.4 games, subtly outpacing Ronaldo, who clinches a trio of goals every 19.1 games. It's a razor-thin margin that speaks volumes about their relentless scoring drives.

Drilling down into their league performances, Ronaldo edges ahead with 42 hat tricks, compared to Messi's 36 in league games. But the Champions League stage tells a different story, where they are deadlocked with 8 hat tricks each, showcasing their knack for shining on the biggest stages.

In this breathtaking race of hat trick hauls, it's a spectacle of scoring supremacy. Ronaldo may lead in total count, but Messi's slightly more frequent hat trick habit adds an extra layer of awe to this fascinating face-off.

Trophy Titans

In the world of individual football accolades, Messi and Ronaldo have redefined excellence, maintaining an elite level unmatched in history. Their grip on the prestigious Ballon d'Or is nothing short of legendary, with Messi outshining with 8 golden orbs, surpassing Ronaldo's impressive haul of 5. It's a record-breaking saga, considering no other player has won more than 3 in the award's history. Imagine a world where they weren't competing against each other - we might have seen either Messi or Ronaldo with 10 or more Ballon d'Ors!

Switching to UEFA's top honors, Ronaldo showcases his award-winning versatility, leading with 4 prestigious awards, including 1 UEFA Club Footballer of the Year, 2 UEFA Best Player in Europe, and 1 UEFA Men's Player of the Year. Messi, not far behind, has claimed 3 such accolades.

When it comes to being the top scorer, Messi has claimed the European Golden Shoe 6 times out of his 8 times finishing as the league's top scorer. Ronaldo, demonstrating his scoring prowess across leagues, has been the top scorer 5 times, securing 4 European Golden Shoes.

Ronaldo also boasts the Puskas award for the year's best goal, a feat Messi, despite 7 nominations, has yet to achieve.

However, Messi shines bright on the global stage, having won the Golden Ball at the World Cup twice - a testament to his impact in leading his team to the final in 2014 and triumphing in 2022. Additionally, he's been crowned Copa America's Best Player twice and Best Young Player once.

In this glittering galaxy of individual awards, Messi and Ronaldo each hold their own, with Messi dominating the Ballon d'Or count, while Ronaldo showcases a wider range of top-tier accolades.

Silverware Scorecard

In the glittering world of football trophies, Messi and Ronaldo have both etched their names in gold, but it's Messi who takes the lead in the overall trophy count. He boasts a staggering 44 trophies, including a memorable 2008 Olympic gold and the 2005 U-20 World Cup victory, outshining Ronaldo's also impressive collection of 35.

On the international stage, Messi has reached the pinnacle with Argentina, clinching both the coveted Copa America and the illustrious World Cup. Ronaldo, a titan with Portugal, has tasted European glory with the Euros victory and added the Nations League trophy to his cabinet.

Domestically, Messi's trophy cabinet brims with 12 league titles, compared to Ronaldo's 7. However, when it comes to the grand stage of the Champions League, Ronaldo edges ahead with 5 triumphs, just surpassing Messi's 4.

The margin may be narrow, but in terms of sheer numbers, Messi currently takes the top spot in this trophy tally. Both have amassed an enviable array of silverware, but Messi's breadth of victories gives him a slight edge in this round of their storied rivalry.

Record Rumble

In the realm of record-setting, Messi and Ronaldo are in a league of their own, each boasting a plethora of records that underline their extraordinary careers. They stand shoulder to shoulder in terms of the sheer number of records held, but the nature of their achievements offers a fascinating contrast.

Messi's record-breaking prowess is highlighted by his otherworldly feat of scoring 91 goals in a single calendar year (2012), a feat so astounding it secured him a spot in the Guinness World Records. To give context to this astronomical number, Messi's next best tally was 60 goals, while Ronaldo's peak hit 69.

Ronaldo, on the other hand, is the undisputed king of the Champions League records. He leads with the most goals, assists, free kick goals, and boasts the most hat-tricks (a record he shares with Messi), as well as the most goals in a single Champions League season.

Messi reigns supreme in Europe at the domestic level, setting records for the most league goals in a single season (50 goals) and scoring in the most consecutive league matches (21 matches, netting 33 goals).

On the international front, Ronaldo shines as the all-time top scorer with a staggering 128 goals, while Messi holds the title of the highest-scoring South American with 106 goals.

In this battle of records, it's a showcase of Messi's scoring frenzy and Ronaldo's Champions League mastery, each setting benchmarks that echo their unique styles and strengths.

International Icons

At the international stage, Messi and Ronaldo have both carved out extraordinary careers, albeit not quite as otherworldly as their club-level exploits, yet still undeniably impressive.

Ronaldo, Portugal's goal machine, strikes every 127 minutes, while Messi, Argentina's talisman, finds the net every 141 minutes. Delving into overall contributions, Ronaldo makes his mark every 100 minutes, but Messi edges ahead slightly with a contribution every 94 minutes.

Ronaldo reigns as Portugal's all-time leading scorer with an awe-inspiring 128 goals in 205 appearances. Messi, not far behind, holds the mantle of Argentina's top scorer with 106 goals in 180 games.

Their individual accolades on the international scene further highlight their impact. Ronaldo claimed the Euro 2021 Golden Boot and the Euro 2016 Silver Boot. Messi, on the other hand, has twice lifted the World Cup Golden Ball (2014 and 2022), the only player ever to achieve this feat, and has twice been named Copa America's Best Player (2015 and 2021). He also clinched the Golden Boot at Copa America 2021 and the Silver Boot at the 2022 World Cup.

Messi's journey with Argentina has seen its share of ups and downs, enduring heartbreak in four major finals before triumphing in the Copa America 2021, the 2022 Finalissima against Italy, and the ultimate glory -

winning the World Cup. His cabinet also boasts an Olympic Gold and a FIFA U20 World Cup trophy.

Ronaldo, too, has had his moments of glory and disappointment, winning the 2016 European Championships with Portugal and the UEFA Nations League, while experiencing a loss in the Euro 2004 final. He also holds the record for the most goals in international football history.

In summary, while Ronaldo leads in goalscoring prowess, Messi's array of individual awards, including four Best Player awards at major tournaments (the most in history), along with his victories in both the Copa America and World Cup, paint a picture of two supremely talented individuals, each with their own remarkable story on the international stage.

Thank you for reading!

If you've enjoyed this dive into the fascinating world of Messi and Ronaldo, others like you will too! Help fellow football fans discover this treasure trove of facts and trivia:

Scan the QR Code Below: It takes you directly to our Amazon page.

Leave a Review: Share what you loved and why others should read it.

Your review is a game-changer – it guides and inspires fellow football enthusiasts. Thank you for being an amazing supporter of this journey!